The Fundamentals of Typography
Gavin Ambrose/Paul Harris

Windsor and Maidenhead

ava
academia

An AVA Book

Published by AVA Publishing SA
Rue des Fontenailles 16
Case Postale
1000 Lausanne 6
Switzerland
Tel: +41 786 005 109
Email: enquiries@avabooks.com

Distributed by Thames & Hudson (ex-North America)
181a High Holborn
London WC1V 7QX
United Kingdom
Tel: +44 20 7845 5000
Fax: +44 20 7845 5055
Email: sales@thameshudson.co.uk
www.thamesandhudson.com

Distributed in the USA & Canada by:
Ingram Publisher Services Inc.
1 Ingram Blvd.
La Vergne TN 37086
USA
Tel: +1 866 400 5351
Fax: +1 800 838 1149
Email: customer.service@ingrampublisherservices.com

English Language Support Office
AVA Publishing (UK) Ltd.
Tel: +44 1903 204 455
Email: enquiries@avabooks.com

Second edition © AVA Publishing SA 2011
First published in 2006

ISBN 978-2-940411-76-4

Library of Congress Cataloging-in-Publication Data
Ambrose, Gavin; Harris, Paul.
The Fundamentals of Typography / Gavin Ambrose, Paul Harris p. cm.
Includes bibliographical references and index.
ISBN: 9782940411764 (pbk.:alk.paper)
eISBN: 9782940447244
1.Graphic design (Typography).2.Graphic arts.
Z246 .A547 2011

10 9 8 7 6 5 4 3 2 1

Design by Gavin Ambrose

Production by AVA Book Production Pte. Ltd., Singapore
Tel: +65 6334 8173
Fax: +65 6259 9830
Email: production@avabooks.com.sg

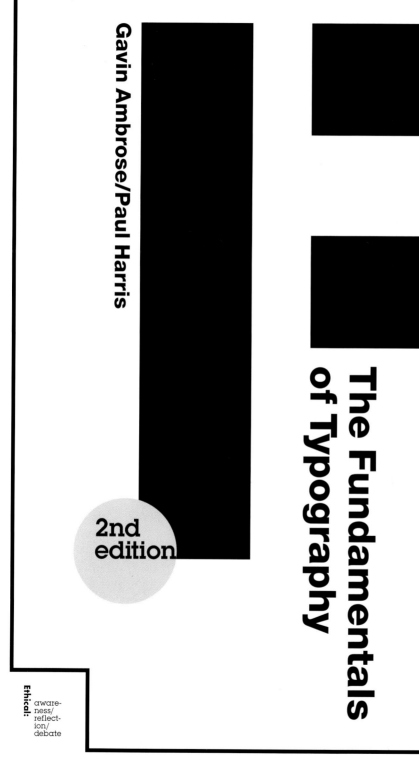

Gavin Ambrose/Paul Harris

The Fundamentals
of Typography

2nd
edition

Ethical: aware-
ness/
reflect-
ion/
debate

academia

contents

introduction

'Language is the dress
of thought.'

Samuel Johnson

Typography surrounds us: it adorns the buildings and the streets through which we pass, it is a component part of the ever-expanding variety of media we consume – from magazines, to television and the Internet – and we even increasingly sport it on our clothing in the form of branding and symbolic messages.

The typography that is a fundamental part of our lives today is the culmination of centuries of development, as the letters that comprise the written word evolved and crystallized into the alphabets that are in common usage. Technology has played a central role in this development, affecting and changing the way that the marks we recognize as characters are made and presented. Through the development of the printing industry, technology gave birth to the concept of typography, the many different presentations of the same character set.

While this book provides a deep insight into the essence of typographical development from the base of its historical roots, it goes much further, as by necessity it deals with language and communication, two concepts to which typography is inextricably linked. As the eighteenth-century English writer Samuel Johnson said, *'Language is the dress of thought'*. That being the case, typography can be viewed as one of the swatches of fabric from which that dress is made.

It is hoped that this book will serve as a valuable source of typographical information with which informed design choices can be made, to add depth and context to a work. This book is also intended to be a source of creative inspiration through the visual exploration of typefaces over the ages.

a — American Typewriter Light

B — Busorama

C — Century Gothic

d — De Vinne

E — Empire

f — Wittenberger Fraktur MT

g — Georgia

h — Humanist 777

i — Impact

j — Joanna

k — Kis

l — Linear Konstrukt

m — Modern No. 20

n — News Gothic

o — Onyx

P — Perpetua

q — Quorum Black

R — Rosewood

s — Stop

t — Trixie Cameo

u — Univers 45

v — VAG Rounded

w — Windsor

x — Xoxoxa

y — Yorstat

Z — Zapfino

There are thousands of fonts available and used throughout the world and they each have a story to tell. This simple A-Z presentation of some of the rich and diverse variety of typefaces demonstrates the many nuances, styles, historical and cultural references that typography includes.

'Typography at its best
is a visual form of language
linking timelessness and
time.'

Robert Bringhurst

chapter 1
type and language

Typography has developed over the last 600 years as the printing process has evolved. The characters that are printed, however, have been developed over a much longer time period as language itself has developed from Egyptian hieroglyphs to the Latin letters we use today.

This chapter looks at the history of typography in relation to the development of language together with the cultural and historical changes the world has undergone. Typography is not only a craft, it is also part of a wider context. Having an understanding of this context can help to inform and enrich typographic practice.

Type and language

Type is the means by which an idea is written and given visual form. Many typefaces in use today are based upon designs created in earlier historical epochs, and the characters themselves have a lineage that extends back thousands of years to the first mark-making by primitive man, when characters were devised to represent objects or concepts.

This section is an introduction to the complex origins of type. An appreciation of typography naturally involves understanding how written language developed. A general timeline is presented here but it is important to remember that there is overlap across epochs and for many major developments, there exist counter-claims to the invention. What is shown here serves as a guide to the major milestones in typography.

This section aims to be as comprehensive as possible, but it is impossible to be conclusive. One of the wonders of typography is this fluidity, its ability to adapt to circumstances, technological advances and cultural shifts. For simplicity, this section has been divided into the following categories; The alphabet, Early printing, 1800s, Arts and Crafts Movement, The early twentieth century, 1950s, 1960s, 1970s, 1980s, 1990s and Graphic design since 2000.

Language is not static

Letters, language and indeed typography develop and change over time as the dominant power inherits, alters, adapts and imposes its will on existing forms. The modern Latin alphabet is a result of such ongoing transition having been developed and adapted over several millennia.

For example, the modern letter 'A' was originally a pictogram representing an ox's head, but as the Phoenicians wrote from right to left, the symbol was turned on its side. Under the Greeks, who wrote from left to right, it was turned again and finally, the Romans turned the character full-circle, giving it the form that we recognize today.

A pictogram of an ox's head…

…has been turned on its side by the Phoenicians…

…rotated by the Greeks…

…and turned upright by the Romans, to form the modern 'A'.

THE ALPHABET

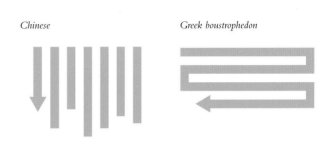

Latin   *Arabic*   *Chinese*   *Greek boustrophedon*

Reading direction
The direction in which text is read varies from
language to language and is determined in part by
historical factors such as how text used to be written.

For example, Chinese calligraphers use paint brushes
to draw ideograms and so it is easier to write down the
page with the right hand, while controlling the scroll
with the left.

Cuneiform tablets
Cuneiform uses a wedge-shaped stylus to make impressions into a wet clay tablet and is one
of the earliest standardized writing systems. It was developed in ancient Mesopotamia, the
region that is now east of the Mediterranean, from about 4,000 BC until about 100 BC. Early
forms of cuneiform were written in columns from top to bottom, but later changed to be
written in rows from left to right. With this change the cuneiform signs were turned on their
sides. Cuneiform began to die out as other language systems such as Aramaic spread through
the region in the seventh and sixth centuries BC, and as the use of Phoenician script increased.

Some terms to be familiar with
There are many terms used within this book that you'll need to be familiar with, many of which are often confused.

PHONOGRAM
A written symbol, letter, character or other mark that
represents a sound, syllable, morpheme or word.

SYMBOL
A graphic element that communicates the ideas and
concepts that it represents rather than denoting what
it actually is.

IDEOGRAM
A graphic element that represents an idea or a concept.

PICTOGRAM
A graphic element that describes an action or series
of actions through visual references or clues.

ICON
A graphic element that represents an object, person or
something else.

Hieroglyphs

Hieroglyphs use a pictogrammatic writing system and were used by several cultures including the Ancient Egyptians and Incas. Each pictogram represents an object rather than a vocal sound. There are over 750 individual Egyptian pictograms. Hieroglyphs can be written from right to left, left to right, or downwards. This is indicated in each piece of text by the direction in which the objects face. For example, if they are facing to the left, the inscription is read from left to right. Border lines are used to indicate that text should be read from top to bottom.

Hieroglyphs on papyrus, reading downwards, as indicated by the border lines (above left).

The Rosetta Stone (above right) was carved in 196 BC with an inscription in Egyptian hieroglyphs, demotic and Greek. Discovered in 1799, the three scripts were key in deciphering hieroglyphics.

These Chinese ideograms represent the four seasons (left to right) spring, summer, autumn and winter.

Ideogram-based languages

Ideogrammatic languages use characters or symbols to represent ideas or concepts. They have a one-to-one relation between a symbol and an idea. Ideogrammatic languages, traditionally written down the page, include Chinese, Japanese, Korean and Thai.

Chinese and Japanese scripts

Written Chinese assigns a single distinctive symbol, or character, to each word. Many symbols have remained fundamentally the same for over 3,000 years even though the writing system has been standardized and stylistically altered. The system became word-based to express abstract concepts, with ideograms representing sounds rather than concepts.

A Japanese writing system emerged in the fourth century, appropriating Kanji characters from Chinese for their phonetic rather than semantic value. Alongside Kanji, three 'Kana' scripts emerged. These syllabic scripts are Hiragana, Katakana and Romaji, (used for words borrowed from Western languages or where computer software does not accommodate Japanese script).

  ワタシ **Watashi** I

Kanji　　　　*Hiragana*　　　　*Katakana*　　　　*Romaji*　　　　*English*

Phoenician characters

The Phoenicians lived in the eastern Mediterranean regions. They developed what was to become the basis of the modern Latin alphabet in around 1600 BC through a system of 22 'magic signs' or symbols that represented sounds rather than objects.

The symbols could be put together in different combinations to construct thousands of words, even though the alphabet only contained consonants. Phoenician was written horizontally from right to left without spaces between words, although dots were sometimes used to denote word breaks.

The 22 magic signs

The Phoenicians were responsible for the development of what is arguably the greatest invention in humanity.

The alphabet of 22 magic signs is pictured below along with its Latin equivalent and the objects that each character is believed to have originally represented.

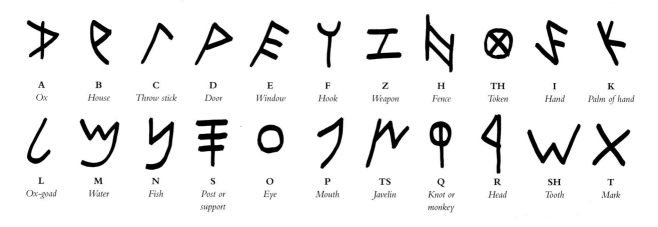

A	**B**	**C**	**D**	**E**	**F**	**Z**	**H**	**TH**	**I**	**K**
Ox	*House*	*Throw stick*	*Door*	*Window*	*Hook*	*Weapon*	*Fence*	*Token*	*Hand*	*Palm of hand*

L	**M**	**N**	**S**	**O**	**P**	**TS**	**Q**	**R**	**SH**	**T**
Ox-goad	*Water*	*Fish*	*Post or support*	*Eye*	*Mouth*	*Javelin*	*Knot or monkey*	*Head*	*Tooth*	*Mark*

Some terms to be familiar with

Linguistics – the study of language – uses the following terms to describe various elements of language and speech.

Phoneme

The basic sound units used to form words. For example, the phonemes 'o' and 'x' come together to make the word 'ox'. The pronunciation of letters varies, so there are more phonemes than letters.

Morpheme

Phoneme group forming the smallest language unit. Each morpheme has a meaning, for example 'discredited' has three; 'dis', 'credit' and 'ed'.

DIS   CREDIT   ED

Syllable

A unit of spoken language consisting of a single, uninterrupted sound. The word 'discredited' has four syllables.

DIS   CRED   IT   ED

Letter

A letter is a mark or glyph (symbol) used in an alphabetic writing system to indicate a sound. A letter's context dictates its pronunciation

D I S C R E D I T E D

The Greek alphabet

The Greeks adopted characters from the Phoenician system (such as aleph (a) and beth (b)) and used them to develop their own alphabet. (Indeed, the word alphabet is derived from the Greek alpha (a) and beta (b).) By around 800 BC the Greeks had added other characters to their alphabet, and this became the basis of the modern-day Hebrew and Arabic scripts. Early Greek was written in the boustrophedon style (*see below*) where rather than proceeding from left to right as in modern English, or right to left as in Arabic, alternate lines must be read in opposite directions.

Aleph Beth
Alpha Beta
AlphaBeta
Alphabet

α	Alpha	η	Eta	ν	Nu	τ	Tau
β	Beta	θ	Theta	ξ	Xi or Si	υ	Upsilon
γ	Gamma	ι	Iota	ο	Omicron	φ	Phi
δ	Delta	κ	Kappa	π	Pi	χ	Chi
ε	Epsilon	λ	Lambda	ρ	Rho	ψ	Psi
ζ	Zeta	μ	Mu	σ	Sigma	ω	Omega

The 24 characters from the modern Greek alphabet and their Greek names.

Vowels and spaces

The Greeks developed vowels, which created a complete and flexible phonetic alphabet. The first vowel letters were **A** (alpha), **E** (epsilon), **I** (iota), **O** (omicron), and **Υ** (upsilon). The origins of modern Latin vowels can clearly be seen. Greek and Latin manuscripts were originally written with no spacing between words, as shown below.

ItwascommonforGreektobewrittenwithnospacing.

The insertion of spaces between words and diacritical marks (see page 75) was a development that helped facilitate reading and comprehension.

Boustrophedon writing

Text written boustrophedonically moves across the page from left to right, drops down a line and then comes back from right to left. There are three methods of doing this: reversing the lines, reversing the lines and words, or reversing the lines, words and letters.

The Cyrillic alphabet

The Cyrillic alphabet is based on Glagolitic (developed by missionaries during the ninth century) and Greek. Developed in the tenth century, it is widely used in Slavic languages such as Belarusian, Bulgarian, Macedonian, Russian, Serbian and Ukrainian. The Cyrillic alphabet has 33 letters, including 21 consonants and ten vowels, and two letters without sounds that represent hard and soft signs. Some Cyrillic characters are shown below, along with their Greek equivalents.

Б

The Cyrillic letter Be is derived from the Greek letter Beta (β).

Д

The Cyrillic letter De is derived from the Greek letter Delta (δ).

З

The Cyrillic letter Ze is derived from the Greek letter Zeta (ζ).

Ж

Some characters, such as Zhe, have no similar letter in Greek or Latin.

The Russian alphabet

The 33 Russian Cyrillic lower-case and upper-case letters are shown with their English transliteration.

а	А	**a**	и	И	**i**	с	С	**s**	ъ	Ъ	**"**
б	Б	**b**	й	Й	**j**	т	Т	**t**	ы	Ы	**y**
в	В	**v**	к	К	**k**	у	У	**u**	ь	Ь	**'**
г	Г	**g**	л	Л	**l**	ф	Ф	**f**	э	Э	**eh**
д	Д	**d**	м	М	**m**	х	Х	**kh**	ю	Ю	**yu**
е	Е	**e**	н	Н	**n**	ц	Ц	**ts**	я	Я	**ya**
ё	Ё	**e**	о	О	**o**	ч	Ч	**ch**			
ж	Ж	**zh**	п	П	**p**	ш	Ш	**sh**			
з	З	**z**	р	Р	**r**	щ	Щ	**shch**			

Semitic and Aramaic languages

Aramaic developed from Phoenician in around 900 BC in what is modern-day Syria and south-east Turkey. It is a Semitic language and a precursor for Arabic and Hebrew, which it closely resembles.

Aramaic was used and spread by the Assyrian empire and the Babylonian and Persian empires that followed it, taking the language as far as India and Ethiopia. Note the similarities with the original Phoenician symbols shown on page 13.

The 22 characters of the Aramaic alphabet and their Latin equivalents.

Arabic

Modern-day Arabic, like Phoenician, is written and read from right to left. Arabic is based on the 22 consonants of the Phoenician alphabet with an optional marking of vowels using diacritics. Arabic script uses the Aramaic letter names (Alef, Jeem, Dal, Zai, Sheen, and so on).

This alphabet contains 18 letter shapes but by adding one, two, or three diacritical marks (representing vowel sounds) to these letters, a total of 28 letters is obtained. These diacritical marks originate in Hebrew and Aramaic and were added so that Muslims of non-Arab origin could correctly pronounce the Koran.

ا	ب	ت	ث	ج	ح	خ	ر	ذ	د	ز	س	ش	ص	ض
a	b	t	th	j	h	kh	d	dh	r	z	s	sh	s	d

ط	ظ	ع	غ	ف	ق	ك	ل	م	ن	ه	و	ي
t	z	c	gh	f	q	k	l	m	n	h	w	y

The Roman alphabet

The 26-letter Roman alphabet that we use today was formed from the Greek alphabet and spread through the Roman empire. Majuscules or upper-case letters derive directly from the forms carved in stone by the Romans, and these are the basis for many modern-day typefaces.

Roman is now also frequently used to describe basic letterforms, principally the minuscules (lower-case letters), even though the name is derived from the majuscule forms. The Romans also used seven of their letterforms as base numerals, with each letter representing a numeric building block as pictured below.

I	V	X	L	C	D	M
1	5	10	50	100	500	1000

LIKETHEEARLIERGREEKALPHABETOFTENNOSPACEWASUSEDBETWEENWORDS
BUT·OFTEN·A·DOT· CHARACTER·WAS·USED·INSTEAD

Trajan, Carol Twombly, 1989
Modern typefaces such as Trajan (above) have their roots in stone carving from the Roman era. Typographer Twombly was influenced by early Roman forms in this design, which is modern yet steeped in historical reference.

The ampersand

The ampersand character is a ligature of the letters of the Latin word *et*, which means 'and'. The name 'ampersand' is a contraction of the phrase 'and per se and', which translates as 'the symbol for and by itself means and'. The 'e' and 't' can still be clearly seen in many ampersand characters, as shown opposite.

The modern Latin alphabet

The modern Latin alphabet consists of 52 upper- and lower-case letters with ten numerals and a variety of other symbols, punctuation marks and accents that are employed by various different languages. Lower-case letters developed from cursive (joined up) versions of the upper-case letters.

ABCDEFGHIJKLMNOPQRSTUVWXYZabcde
ghijklmnopqrstuvwxyz1234567890§-=[];'\`,./
%^&*()_+{}:"|~<>?¡#¢¶•—≠Œ®†¥Ø"'…
Æ«Ç÷ÅÄÊÎÔÛØUÁÉÍÓÚåäêîôûøuáéíóú

All alphabets are not the same

Although most European alphabets are Latin based they are not all the same.

English has 26 letters, while traditional Spanish has 30 with the addition of 'ñ', 'll', 'ch', 'rr'. Italian has only 21 letters, and lacks 'j', 'k', 'w', 'x' and 'y'.

ABCDEFGHILMNOPQRSTUVZ

The modern Italian alphabet lacks the letters 'j', 'k', 'w', 'x' and 'y'.

The 0

Modern numbers derive from Arabic characters and their adoption brought the '0' with them. The numerals themselves originated in India and came into use in Arabic around AD 1000. Common usage in Europe did not occur until the Renaissance period. Modern European digits were created in India in the sixth century or earlier, and were introduced to the West by Arab scholars. As they represent place-based values and have a zero, calculations can be performed with relative ease (how quickly can you add up the roman numerals?). Another advantage is that numbers of infinite length can be formed, whereas Roman numerals soon meet with limitations.

M	1000
C	100
VI	6
IV	4

Gutenberg

Johannes Gutenberg (c.1400-1468) was a German printer who developed the first printing press and the use of movable type. The development of the printing press allowed the mass production of books.

Movable type further improved this development by allowing text characters to be reused, providing further time and cost savings. This technology remained the basis of the printing industry until hot metal printing.

Movable type

Shown is a piece of movable type. Many typographical terms are named after the different characteristics of these type blocks. The physical dimensions of the block dictated spacing and made negative spacing impossible, whereas computer technology makes spacing more flexible. While digitized type still adheres to the same conventions of the bounding box (pictured far right) in terms of measurements, digitization allows these boxes to overlap, and indeed have negative tracking.

Blackletter

Block, Blackletter, Gothic, Old English, black or broken typefaces are based on the ornate writing style prevalent during the Middle Ages. Nowadays these typefaces appear heavy and difficult to read in large text blocks due to the complexity of the letters and the fact that they seem antiquated and unfamiliar to us. Blackletter typefaces are commonly used to add decorative touches such as initial caps.

Blackletter 686
Blackletter 686, a modern font created by Bitstream Inc. and based on London Text scripts from the Middle Ages that were written with feather quills. The clean lines of this font result in an engraved effect.

The effect of printing in Europe

As printing spread it gave rise to various typographical styles. Many printers adopted the Venetian model as interest in Italian Renaissance art and culture grew. Parisian printer Claude Garamond (c.1480-1561) established the first independent type foundry.

Letterforms from this period utilized the greater detail that working with metal offered. Old Style typeforms superseded Blackletter as people in Renaissance Europe began to favour classical forms. These are more condensed than the Carolingian forms that preceded them, but more rounded than Blackletter. Some common fonts are shown on the opposite page with an explanation of their development and characteristics.

ABCDEFGHIJKLMNOPQRSTUVWXYZ

Bembo

Created by Monotype in 1929 for a Stanley Morison project, Bembo is an Old Style font based on a Roman face cut by Francisco Griffo da Bologna, which Aldus Manutius used to print Pietro Bembo's 1496 publication of *De Aetna*. Morison modified letterforms such as the 'G' to create a typeface with 31 weights – an all-purpose font family suitable for almost any application. Note the crossed strokes in the 'W'.

ABCDEFGHIJKLMNOPQRSTUVWXYZ

Garamond

Based on designs by seventeenth-century French printer Jean Jannon that were themselves based on typefaces cut by Claude Garamond from the sixteenth century, Garamond is an Aldine font (fonts based on the designs of Aldus Manutius in the fifteenth century, of which Bembo and Garamond are examples) that is elegant and readable. Note the crossed strokes in the 'W', and the bowl of the 'P' that does not reach the stem.

ABCDEFGHIJKLMNOPQRSTUVWXYZ

Janson

Created c.1685 by Hungarian punchcutter Miklós Kis, Janson wrongly bears the name of Dutch punchcutter Anton Janson to whom it was formerly attributed. The font has sturdy forms and strong stroke contrast. Note the long tail of the 'Q', the oval shape of the 'O' and the unified apex of the 'W'.

ABCDEFGHIJKLMNOPQRSTUVWXYZ

Caslon Antique

This is a modern font based on a historical font. Modern typographers' attempts to recreate ancient fonts in digital format often involve imaginative leaps, as they are based on printed texts where there is ink spread, and in many cases the original fonts are not available to work from.

ABCDEFGHIJKLMNOPQRSTUVWXYZ *vw*

Caslon

Created in 1725 by typographer William Caslon, this serif font was styled on seventeenth-century Dutch designs. The font can be identified as most Caslons have a capital 'A' with a scooped-out apex, a capital 'C' with two full serifs, and in the italic, a swashed lower-case 'v' and 'w'.

ABCDEFGHIJKLMNOPQRSTUVWXYZ

Baskerville

Created by John Baskerville in the eighteenth century, Baskerville is a versatile transitional font (making it a precursor to the modern faces that followed) with high contrast forms that are used for both body text and display type. Note the absence of the middle serif on the 'W' and the distinctive capital 'Q'.

The Industrial Revolution

The Industrial Revolution brought mechanization, which allowed printing to speed up. Photo-engraving, which replaced handmade printing plates and line-casting machines that revolutionized typesetting also allowed for ever-increasing levels of detail and intricacy.

Technological development also meant that font creation took less time, and this opened the doors for the development of a wider range of typefaces.

One development of the time was the introduction of **BOLDFACE,** used for adding emphasis or hierarchy. Experimentation with serifs saw them become thinner and thinner until they ultimately disappeared. William Caslon's great grandson William Caslon IV cut the first sans serif font in 1816, called English Egyptian. Transitional fonts from this period typically have horizontal serifs, vertical stress and more contrast than Old Style typefaces.

GROTESQUE & GOTHIC

The first sans serif typeface, 1816

William Caslon developed a sans serif typeface called Egyptian in reference to public interest in Egypt following Napoleon's campaign. It was not well received, however, and was called 'grotesque' and 'Gothic' (a style of architecture going through a revival at the time).

Although Egyptian was originally a sans serif style of font, it has since come to refer to slab serif typefaces, perhaps because the slabs mirror the construction of the pyramids. Other terms for sans serif fonts including Doric and Antique (the French term for sans serif) are now used less, but are still in use as shown below.

Doric, Walter Tracy, 1973

Based on the earlier woodblock designs, this sans serif font retains some of the original characteristics and weight of the original typeface.

ANTIQUE OLIVE

Antique Olive, Roger Excoffon, 1962-1966

Using the french term, this sans serif has distinctive characters such as the 'Q' and an exaggerated inner apex on the 'A'.

Commercial art

Lithography was invented in Austria by Alois Senefelder in 1796. Following refinements, by 1848 the process enabled print speeds of 10,000 sheets per hour, making mass production of designs economically viable. Lithography allowed the merging of art with industry to produce posters and colour plates for books.

The first person to mass produce posters with lithography was Jules Chéret (1836-1933) in Paris. Other early protagonists include Thomas Theodor Heine (1867-1948) and Henri de Toulouse-Lautrec (1864-1901). Despite these developments, the term 'graphic design' does not appear until the 1950s.

THE ARTS AND CRAFTS MOVEMENT

The Victorian Arts and Crafts Movement (1850s) developed as a rejection of heavily ornamented interiors with many pieces of furniture, collections of ornamental objects and surfaces covered with fringed cloths.

The Arts and Crafts Movement favoured simplicity, good craftsmanship and design. British artist and architect William Morris was a leading exponent of this new style that sought to re-establish a link between beautiful work and the worker.

Franklin Gothic, Morris Fuller Benton, 1904
Franklin Gothic was named after Benjamin Franklin. Morris Fuller Benton's design of 1904 is still popular today, appearing in many newspapers and as a headline typeface for advertising.

Copperplate Gothic, Frederic W. Goudy, 1901
Copperplate Gothic exhibits some of the attention to detail found in the Arts and Crafts Movement.

Kelmscott is a typeface designed by renowned architect and designer, William Morris. It is named after the house in which he lived between 1878 and 1896 and was used in early books produced by the Kelmscott Press.

Modernism

Modernism, through the cubist, surrealist and Dadaist movements was shaped by the industrialization and urbanization of Western society. Modernists departed from the rural and provincial zeitgeist prevalent in the Victorian era.

Functionality and progress became key concerns in the attempt to move beyond the external physical representation of reality. Modernist typefaces often sought to force viewers to see the everyday differently by presenting unfamiliar forms.

De Stijl

An art and design movement evolved from the magazine of the same name that was founded by Theo Van Doesburg. De Stijl used strong rectangular forms, employed primary colours and celebrated asymmetrical compositions.

Constructivism

A modern art movement originating in Moscow in 1920, characterized by the use of industrial materials to create non-representational, often geometric objects. Russian constructivism translated to graphic design through a use of black and red sans serif type arranged in asymmetrical blocks.

The Bauhaus

The Bauhaus opened in 1919 under the direction of renowned architect Walter Gropius. Until forced to close in 1933, the Bauhaus sought to initiate a fresh approach to design following the First World War, with a focus on functionality rather than adornment.

Left

In 1923 Wassily Kandinsky proposed a universal relationship between the three basic shapes and the three primary colours: the yellow triangle was the most active and dynamic, and the blue circle cold and passive.

bayer universal b̲ʌsik ʌlfʌbet

Bayer Universal, Herbert Bayer, 1925

Herbert Bayer embodied the modernist desire to reduce designs to as few elements as possible and repeatedly experimented with typography to reduce the alphabet to a single case.

Basic Alphabet was a further experimentation with language. Words are written as they sound, with silent letters dropped and typographical elements reduced. Capitals are indicated with an underscore, for example.

Dadaism

An artistic and literary movement (1916-1923) that developed following the First World War and sought to discover an authentic reality through the abolition of traditional culture and aesthetic forms. Dadaism brought new ideas, materials and directions, but with little uniformity. Its principles were of deliberate irrationality, anarchy and cynicism, and the rejection of laws of beauty. Dadaists lived in the moment and for the moment. The name Dada derives from the French for hobby horse.

Dada, Richard Kegler, 1995–1998

Inspired by Dada typography and poetry, Richard Kegler created Dada according to the principles of irrationality and anarchic arrangement so that there appears to be little congruence from one letter to the next.

BASED ON ENGRAVINGS

Perpetua, Eric Gill, 1928

Gill based this design on characters from old engravings. Small diagonal serifs and a medieval number set add an element of formality to the typeface.

The constructivist tradition

Futura, Paul Renner, 1927

Futura is considered the major typeface development to come out of the constructivist orientation of the Bauhaus movement. The characters are based on the simple forms of circle, triangle and square, but softened them to be more legible and to create a new, modern type.

BODONI POSTER BOLDFACE

Poster Bodoni, Chauncey H. Griffith, 1929

Based on an eighteenth-century design by Gianbattista Bodoni, this is a modern font characterized by hairline serifs that are subtly bracketed, and heavy downstrokes that give a powerful vertical stress.

23

Following the Second World War a new optimism emerged as a consumer boom erupted in the USA. The cultural scene also expanded, boosted by many European creatives and intellectuals who had fled Nazi Europe. Design became more elaborate, with bright colours that celebrated life – as personified in cars such as the candy-coloured Ford Thunderbird.

The demand for wider choice and the emergence of photosetting helped typography develop. Typographers such as Hermann Zapf led the humanist movement, with the lines between serif and sans serif typefaces blurred as organic lines were reintroduced into typography. Humanist fonts have forms that are based on classic Romans, but without the serifs.

HELVETICA

Created by Max Miedinger in 1957 - the forgotten designer - Helvetica is one of the most famous and popular typefaces in the world. Originally called Haas Grotesk, its name changed to Helvetica in 1960. The Helvetica family has 34 weights and the Neue Helvetica has 51.

UNIVERS

Univers, Adrian Frutiger, 1957

With sturdy, clean forms, Adrian Frutiger's Univers also from 1957 expresses cool elegance and rational competence. It is available in 59 weights that combine well with other fonts.

G G Q Q y y a a

Pictured in black is Helvetica and in green is Univers. Although both are sans serif fonts, there are noticeable differences such as the absence of a tail on the Univers 'G', 'y' and 'a', the more open, rounded counter on the Univers 'a' and the bisecting tail of the Helvetica 'Q'.

International Style (Swiss)
International or Swiss Style was based on the revolutionary principles of the 1920s, such as those devised by De Stijl, Bauhaus and Jan Tschichold's *The New Typography*, which became firmly established in the 1950s. Grids, mathematical principles, minimal decoration and sans serif typography became the norm as typography developed to represent universal usefulness more than personal expression.

OPTIMA – BASED ON THE GOLDEN RATIO

Optima, Hermann Zapf, 1958
Optima was inspired by letters Zapf sketched on two 1,000 lire bank notes, based on grave plates cut c.1530 that he saw while visiting the Santa Croce church in Florence. Optima is a humanist sans serif blended with Roman and calligraphic styles, making it a smooth read and general-purpose font, which became his most successful typeface. Letterforms are in the proportions of the golden ratio.

1960s

The world of culture went pop in the 1960s as music, art, literature and furniture design became more accessible and reflected elements of everyday life. Pop art developed as a reaction against abstract art. It was often witty, purposely obvious and throwaway in its reflection of consumer culture such as advertising and comic books.

Pop art's influence on typography resulted in fonts – particularly for display type – designed or selected according to possible associations or references in place of any particular theory regarding legibility or aesthetics, while the International Style remained influential for body text.

Letraset, 1961

Letraset dry-transfer lettering allowed anyone to do typesetting. Rubbed directly on to artwork or virtually any substrate, it was often used for headlines and display type while body type was supplied via a typewriter. Letraset commissioned new typefaces including Colin Brignall's futuristic Countdown font.

Countdown, Colin Brignall, 1965

This typeface developed for Letraset is synonymous with the 1960s, the space race and the development of computer technology.

OCR-A, Optical Character Recognition, Adrian Frutiger and the USA Bureau of Standards, 1966

OCR-A is a standardized, monospaced font designed for Optical Character Recognition by electronic devices, using standards developed by the American National Standards Institute in 1966 for the processing of documents by banks and credit card companies. The characters fit into a 4 x 7 grid which makes them easily read by a scanner, even though they are not so legible to the human eye. Subsequent version OCR-B was made a world standard in 1973 and is more legible to the human eye.

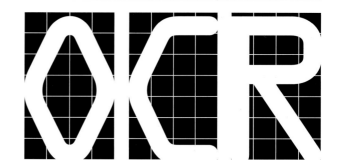

Eurostile

Eurostile, Aldo Novarese, 1962

Eurostile features a subtle distortion of circular sans serif geometric forms, with rounded corners that look like television sets of the time.

Typography in the 1970s continued where the 1960s left off, becoming more decorative, outrageous and extravagant until the middle of the decade, when punk emerged. Punk rejected the decadent, elaborate nature of music, fashion and the visual arts in favour of the disposable and shocking.

ITC

The International Typeface Corp. (ITC) was formed in New York to market new typeface designs, distribute royalties to the creators and extend rights to typographers that were threatened by the photographic copying of fonts. Prior to this, type designers had been tied to particular typesetting machine manufacturers. The formation of the ITC resulted in a drive to collect and commission new work, including revisiting classic fonts.

austrian designer michael neugebauer created cirkulus in 1970 as an experimental display face using combinations of hairline circles and straight lines. the letters have a constructivist feel that is reminiscent of the revolutionary 1920s. cirkulus is a unicase alphabet (there are no upper-case characters), with a very lightweight appearance that is best used in large display sizes.

Early computers and photocomposition

Photocomposition improved in the 1960s and facilitated the copying and production of fonts. By projecting a character created on the screen of a cathode ray tube (like a TV) through a lens on to light-sensitive paper or film, it could be stored in a magnetic memory, overwritten and edited. This was much faster than physically adjusting hot metal type and led to increased proliferation of typefaces and historical revivals as fonts became more international. The 1970s saw computers increasingly involved in this process through a mixture of photocomposition and the digital techniques that would emerge later, with several competing languages and formats. Throughout this decade the potential to design directly on screen increased, offering industry professionals more options and flexibility.

kabel

ITC Kabel, Victor Caruso, 1976

Kabel features basic forms influenced by stone-carved Roman letters that consist of a few pure and clear geometric forms such as circles, squares and triangles. Art Deco elements such as the seemingly awkward angles of some of the curves makes Kabel appear very different from other geometric modernist typefaces. Based on an earlier design by Rudolph Koch in 1923, the typeface is reminiscent of constructivist experiments.

1980s

The 1980s saw the introduction of personal computers, computer games, music videos and desktop publishing, as the invention of the laser printer meant that expensive photosensitive paper was no longer needed. The digital revolution meant that new fonts could be designed and trialled quickly and easily, without the great expense and commitment of hot metal type.

The 'Mac'

Macintosh revolutionized the personal computer in1984 by making computer screens user-friendly and hiding the operational programming from the user, in contrast to IBM's approach. Control in type production migrated away from professional typesetters to designers, and extended to amateurs as well as industry professionals. The low resolution of early personal computers called for new fonts to ensure legibility.

Arial is a contemporary sans serif design that contains many humanist characteristics. The overall treatment of curves is softer and fuller than in most industrial style sans serif faces. Terminal strokes are cut on the diagonal and help to give the face a less mechanical appearance. The typeface was designed in 1982 by Robin Nicholas and Patricia Saunders for Monotype.

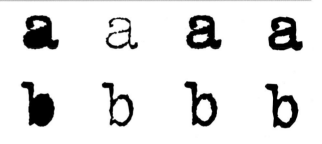

Trixie, LettError, 1989

Trixie was developed at a time when font design turned again towards developing more sophisticated and smoother fonts. LettError based Trixie on the look of a dirty, inky typewriter type to give a rougher look that is irreverent and playful. Dutch company LettError was established by Dutch designers Erik van Blokland and Just van Rossum.

The Face, 1981–2004

Graphic designer Neville Brody revolutionized magazine design with his unabashed love of typography that he displayed on the pages of *The Face*, a style magazine covering music, design and fashion. Historic and contemporary type were subjected to exaggeration in scale and proportion, were exploded and otherwise distorted, and complemented with Brody's own computer-generated fonts as he challenged the notion of legibility.

As the 1990s began, graphic designers reacted to the International Style and sought to break away from the constraints of the grid patterns in favour of experimentation, playful use of type and a more handmade approach. Type use became more expressive – to be part of the message rather than just its conveyor.

FUSE, Neville Brody / Research Studios, 1991
Typography magazine *FUSE*, founded by Neville Brody and John Wozencroft, saw typography explode into uncharted realms as type designers grabbed hold of the 'free reins' that computer technology gave them.

A font that's a sans **and a serif**

Officina, Erik Spiekermann and Schäfer, Ole, 1990
With both serif and sans serif forms, Officina embodies the ideals of efficient office communication, with styling based on traditional typewriters but adapted to modern technology and spaced for legibility.

Designed for low grade printing

Meta, Erik Spiekermann and MetaDesign, 1991
Meta was based on a rejected typeface commissioned by the German Post Office (Bundespost) in 1984. Hailed as the typeface for the 1990s, it is named after Meta Studio, where the new typeface was used.

Flixel, Just van Rossum / FUSE, 1991
Flixel is a dot pattern font that pushes the boundaries of legibility with its unusual forms.

Can You, Phil Baines / FUSE, 1995
This typeface uses key portions of letterforms that challenge the limits of legibility.

A contemporary twist

Mrs Eaves, Zuzana Licko, 1996
Zuzana Licko based the design of Mrs Eaves on the Baskerville font. Licko gave the font ligatures, such as between the 's' and 't', that give it a contemporary twist.

randomness and regradation Beowolf 21
randomness and regradation Beowolf 22
randomness and regradation Beowolf 23

Beowolf, Letterror, 1990

A misspelling of Beowulf, this radical font sees varying degrees of randomness and regradation. The first iteration, released at the end of 1989, went on to see multiple versions released during the 1990s.

Fresh Dialogue / Stefan Sagmeister, 1996

This poster for the American Institute of Graphic Arts features handwritten typography that is placed in seemingly haphazard blocks. Photos of cow tongues form the crossbars of the capital 'F' of Fresh and reversed 'E' at the end of Dialogue.

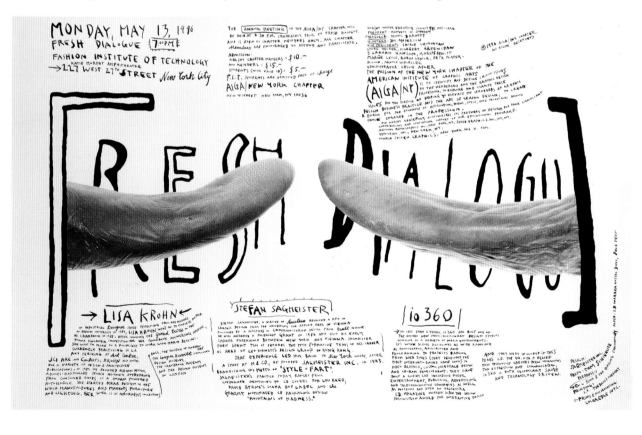

High-resolution digital printing has increased options and challenges in graphic design. The growth of multimedia applications makes new demands on fonts, with the need to obtain legibility between computers, mobile phones and other devices. Graphic designers continue to experiment and enjoy the ability that modern technology allows to free-form type quickly and integrate it in their designs.

Pluralism

Today we are living in a pluralistic phase, embracing the ability to move between different styles and points of view. Rather than there being a single meta-narrative, pluralists suggest that there are many narratives and that fewer universal truths exist in a globalized world. Truths are instead more individualistic, personal and specific. This results in regionalism in graphic design, as something that is appropriate in one country will not necessarily translate well in another.

:DIDOGO

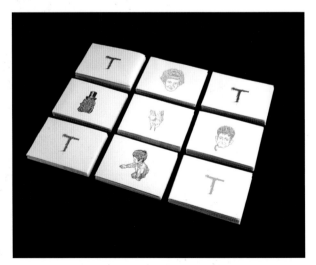

T Bar, George & Vera

This design uses eclectic, almost surreal images including typography that looks like line drawings or etchings.

Didogo, Creasence

This logotype takes direct influence from trends in typography, including the emergence of 'smilies', a form of emoticons, or ASCII art, constructed out of characters of email and text systems. In this example, the colon and the capital 'D' form a simple, smiley face.

Designer as Maker, Studio Myerscough, 2005
Type can be quiet, loud, brash, understated, but ultimately, it can be unexpected. With their freethinking approach to typography, Studio Myerscough demonstrate the power of a simple message.

A Flock of Words, **Why Not Associates and Gordon Young**
Flock of Words is the result of a six-year collaboration, featuring a number of typographic installations as part of a town arts project.

Neutraface, The Design Shop

This brochure was designed by The Design Shop, for the introduction of the Greek version of the font Neutraface, by Cannibal fonts. The designers highlighted the Art Deco characteristics of the font on the front and the back cover. The inners of the brochure feature full-bleed images, and oversized characters, celebrating the font's characteristics. The placement of images on the inner, and the text on the outer, is essentially a reverse of what you would expect, and creates an interesting and elegant design. Having an understanding of the historical and cultural significance of typography helps the designers 'position' the new font in the lineage of letterform development.

'I'm a huge fan of layered, textured typography – there are some amazing type designers at the moment whose work I obsess over but whose processes I simply can't decipher.'

Project description

Lonsdale Boys Club (Loz Curran, Topher Richwhite and Charlie Weaver), commissioned Mercy to develop the graphics for their debut single. The single's name, 'Light Me Up' became the platform for the designers to work from.

In discussion with Doug Mercy, Mercy Liverpool

GA How do you use sketching as a way of developing typography, do you see it as an important part of the design and thinking process?

DM I actually don't use sketchbooks anywhere near as much as I should for general work, but when it comes to a piece of typography it's always my first port of call. I can usually see what it is I want to achieve in my head, but I find I can only physically manifest this through

endlessly doodling it and going through a lot of trial and error (more often than not, because a practical sticking point messes up my idea – in this instance, how to create the three words using one unbroken line without compromising how realistic it would be). Sometimes what looked great in my head just doesn't work in practice – and it is only the process of putting pen to paper that can confirm this.

GA In the Light Me Up project the typography is unexpected, and experimental, do you see this as being part of what designers should be doing? Challenging the boundaries of the medium?

DM Well absolutely designers should be challenging boundaries and experimenting with how they work as a matter of course. But by the same token – if working

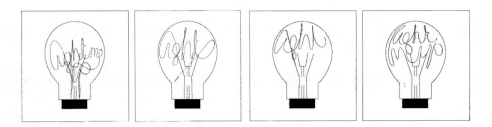

Above and right
Some early development work involved the use of sketching, prior to crafting the final typography.

Right

The raw artwork prior to being
rendered fully into the final cover,
shown overleaf.

commercially at least – we mustn't ever lose sight of why
and where it is appropriate to do so. A lot of designers
can sometimes complain about 'uncreative' clients, but in
a lot of these cases an experimental approach might well
be alienating their customer. There's a time and a place
for everything I guess, and the skill is to know when to
play it straight and when to go that bit further.

GA The result of the Light Me Up project has a strong
sense of craft, in the sense that the typography is 'created',
is this something that is important to you as a designer?
DM I'm a huge fan of crafty, layered, textured
typography – there are some totally amazing type
designers at the moment whose work I obsess over but
whose processes I simply can't decipher. I think that's
great, the idea that even in the days of Macs and quick
fixes, these things still take weeks' of skill and craft to
get just right and mere mortals such as myself can only
marvel at them. But then someone could stick a massive
Helvetica semi-colon up in a gallery and I'd love that too,
so I wouldn't say that I have an exclusive obsession over
hours of craft. If it's right it's right!

Above

The final artwork is a composite of type and image. The design needs to work at a variety of scales within the context of modern music sales. So it needs to be equally successful at a point of sale site (in a store or festival, for example) but it also needs to work online, and on hand-held devices. The final design is immediate, memorable and striking in its simplicity.

TYPOGRAPHY TASK
Typographic 'context'

Premise

We are surrounded by type. We interact with it on a daily basis. It is on the books we read, the signs we follow and the web pages we look at. All of this type has been 'chosen', it has been designed – be it well designed or ill-designed. Every piece of type we interact with has some kind of ancestry, it is descended from an earlier incarnation. Type ranges from the ephemeral to the significant and monumental. The sheer scale results in an imposing structure that conveys a sense of gravity and meaning.

Exercise

1 Over a 24-hour period, collate a record of all the items that you interact with that contain type. This could be signage, packaging, bus tickets, or letters and correspondence.

2 Create an 'audit' of this information. An audit is a quantitative survey of your findings, it is simply looking at what you have found and recording it, you are not at this stage trying to identify any patterns or make any judgements.

3 Start to analyse the information you have gathered. This could be done using some of the following methods:
   - How many touchpoints are with serif as opposed to sans serif type?
   - How many different classifications of type are there, for example Roman, Black letter?
   - How many times do you interact with type?
   - What colours are most popular?
   - What type size is most common?
   - What type of information is it? Is it advertising, public awareness, directional information?
   - What language are these in?

4 Produce a visual outcome of your findings. This could take the form of a series of charts, graphs, diagrams or visualizations. Remember though, that you are trying to present an objective analysis of what you found.

Outcome

To encourage a deeper understanding of the myriad typographic forms that surround us.

'Typography has one plain duty before it and that is to convey information in writing.'

Emil Ruder

chapter 2
a few basics

A discussion of type involves the use of specific terminology relating to its historic characteristics and measurement. An understanding of this terminology and the measurement system is essential for the satisfactory communication of typographical concepts.

Typefaces and fonts

In common usage, the words *typeface* and *font* are used synonymously. In most cases, there is no harm in doing this as the substitution is virtually universal and most people, including designers, would be hard pressed to state each word's true definition.

However, each term possesses a separate and distinct meaning. A typeface is a collection of characters which have the same distinct design, while a font is the physical means of typeface production – be it the description of a typeface in computer code, lithographic film or metal.

James Felici explains the difference as a font being a cookie cutter and the typeface the cookie produced. So while one can ask 'What typeface is that?', a question such as 'What font is that?' when looking at a piece of print or a screen is inaccurate.

What is a font?
A font is the physical means used to create a typeface, whether it be a typewriter, a stencil, letterpress blocks or a piece of PostScript code.

What is a typeface?
A typeface is a collection of characters, letters, numerals, symbols and punctuation, which have the same distinct design.

These are fonts:

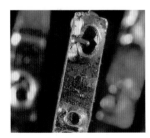  

LWFN

These are typefaces:

A typewriter produces a distinctive typeface, a stencil produces a rough and ready font, letterpress blocks produce richly expressive type, and a computer font containing PostScript information creates a neat and precise typeface.

Typeface anatomy

Typographical characters have an array of attributes and forms
that are described through a variety of different terms, in much the
same way as the different names for every part of the human body.

Apex
The point formed at
the top of a character
such as 'A', where the
left and right strokes
meet.

Beak
The *serif* form at the
end of an *arm*.

Counter
The space inside a
bowl as found on 'e',
'a' and other letters.

Ear
A small stroke
extending from the
the *bowl* of a 'g' or
from the *stem* of let-
ters such as 'r' and 'f'.

Link
A stroke that joins
two other letter parts
such as the *bowls* of a
double-storey 'g'.

Spine
A left-to-right curving
stroke in the 'S' and 's'.

Swash
An elongated curved
entry or exit stroke.

Arm
A horizontal stroke
on the 'T', and 'F' as
well as the upstroke
on the 'K' and 'Y'.
Also called bar.

Bowl
The shape that
encloses a space in
circular letterforms.
The bowl may be
closed or open.

Crossbar
The horizontal
stroke that intersects
the central *stem*.
Also called a *cross
stroke*.

Finial
An ornamental
terminal stroke at the
top of characters such
as the 'a' and 'f'.

Loop
The *bowl* formed by
the tail of a double-
storey 'g'.

Spur
The *terminal* to a *stem*
of a rounded letter.

Tail
The descending stroke
of letters like the 'Q',
'K' and 'R'. The loop
of the 'g' can also be
called a tail.

**Ascenders and
descenders**
Parts of a letter that
extend above the
x-height; or below
the baseline.

Bracket
The transitional
shape, connecting
the *stem* and the
serif.

Cross stroke
A horizontal stroke
that intersects the
central *stem*. Also
called a *crossbar*.

Leg
The lower stroke of
a letter. Sometimes
used for the *tail* of
the 'Q'.

Serif
A small stroke at the
end of a main vertical
or horizontal stroke.

Stem
The main vertical
or diagonal stroke
of a letter.

Terminal
The end of a stroke,
which may take sev-
eral forms such as
acute, flared, concave
and rounded.

Barb
A sharp pointed
serif.

Chin
The angled
terminal of a 'G'.

Crotch
The inner point at
which two angled
strokes meet.

Ligature
Typically a *crossbar*
or *arm* that extends
across a pair of let-
ters to join them.

Shoulder
The curved stroke
leading into the *leg*
of an 'h' or 'n' for
example.

Stress
The orientation,
or slant of a curved
character.

Vertex
The angle formed
at the bottom of a
letter where strokes
meet.

Relative and absolute measurements

Typography uses two types of measurements, *absolute measurements* and *relative measurements*. It is important to understand the differences between these to understand many of the typographic processes.

Absolute measurements

Absolute measurements are easy to understand as they are measurements of fixed values. For example, a millimetre is a precisely defined increment of a centimetre. Equally, points and picas, the basic typographic measurements, have fixed values. All absolute measurements are expressed in finite terms that cannot be altered. Pictured right are four measurement systems that express the same physical distance.

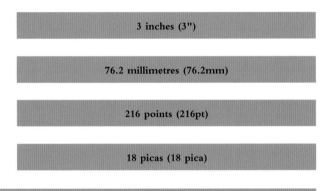

3 inches (3")

76.2 millimetres (76.2mm)

216 points (216pt)

18 picas (18 pica)

Relative measurements

In typography, many measurements, such as character spacing, are linked to type size, which means that their relationships are defined by a series of relative measurements. Ems and ens, for example, are relative measurements that have no prescribed, absolute size. Their size is relative to the size of type that is being set.

Leading is another example of the use of relative measurement. Most desktop publishing programs assign an automatic percentage value for functions like leading. The characters above right are 10pt, so with leading set at 120 percent, they are effectively being set on 12pt leading. As the type gets bigger, so does the leading, as it is relative to the type size. You'll notice that 10pt type on 12pt leading retains whole numbers. However, when you use alternative sizes, by default the leading values sometimes produce irregular numbers, for example 12pt type on 14.4pt leading.

If this did not happen and the leading remained constant, as the characters got bigger they would eventually crash into one another. This is sometimes called negative leading.

10 on 12pt
A standard setting with a regular number for both typesize and leading.

R
R

12 on 14.4pt
Although type has a regular value, the leading now has an irregular number.

R
R

30 on 36pt
Another standard value that has a regular number for both typesize and leading.

R
R

36 on 10pt
Negative leading sees characters overlap – made possible by modern technology.

Points

The point is the unit of measurement used to measure the type size of a font, for example, 7pt Times New Roman. This measurement refers to the height of the type block, not the letter itself as shown below (right). This basic typographical measurement is an absolute measurement equivalent to 1/72 of an inch or 0.35mm and its creation is attributed to French clergyman Sébastien Truchet (1657–1729). It was further developed by Pierre Fournier and Francois Didot in the nineteenth century, before the British/American or Anglo-Saxon point was defined as 1/72 of an inch.

Type sizes traditionally bore a relationship to the 72 point inch (six picas) but with digitized PostScript typefaces, it is now easy to use irregular sizes such as 10.2pt. This relationship is reflected in the old naming system for these common sizes, with 12pt type being referred to as *Pica*. Some of the other names have a looser connection, and indeed the sizes are only approximate translations to the modern point equivalents. These names are no longer in common use, but the equivalent sizes are, with most software packages using these as the default sizes.

Before standardization, typefaces of similar names had varying sizes. A Pica from one type foundry would be exactly 12 points, while the same measurement from another could vary dramatically.

Minion	Bourgeois	Long Primer	Pica	English	Great Primer	2-line Pica	2-line Great Primer	Canon or 4-line
7	9	10	12	14	18	24	36	48

As the point size of a typeface refers to the height of the type block and not the letter itself, different typefaces of the same size behave differently, as these two examples above set in 72pt type show. While they are the same size the characters do not necessarily extend to the top or bottom of the block, which has an impact on leading values discussed on *pages 114–119*. The typefaces shown are Futura (left), and Foundry Sans (right).

The measurement of a piece of movable type is its entire vertical size, not just a measure of the character height.

Picas

A pica is a unit of measurement equal to 12 points that is commonly used for measuring lines of type. There are six picas (or 72 points) in an inch, which is equal to 25.4 millimetres. This is the same for both a traditional pica and a modern PostScript pica. There are six PostScript picas to an inch.

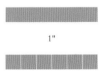

1"

6 Picas

43

The em

The em is a relative unit of measurement used in typesetting to define basic spacing functions, and therefore it is linked to the size of the type. It is a relative measurement in that if the type size increases, so does the size of the em. If the type size decreases, so does the em.

An em equals the size of a given type, i.e. the em of 72pt type is 72 points and the em of 36pt type is 36 points and so on. Although the name of the em implies a relationship to the width of the capital 'M', in reality an 'M' character will rarely be as wide as an em as the illustration (above) demonstrates.

The em is used for defining elements such as paragraph indents and spacing. Different typefaces will produce certain typographical characters whose sizes differ in relation to the em of a given point size. The characters below are 48pt and both therefore have a 48pt em. However, Bembo is clearly 'smaller', and occupies less of the em square than Futura.

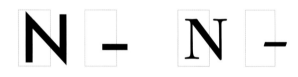

The en

An en is a unit of relative measurement equal to half of one em. In 72pt type, for example, an en would be 36 points. A spaced en rule is often used to denote nested clauses, but it can also be used to mean 'to' in phrases such as 10–11 and 1975–1981.

Characters that extend beyond the em

Although characters rarely fill their em, some special characters such as the per thousand symbol (below, left) extend beyond their em, which may cause a spacing problem.

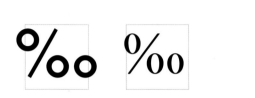

Ems, ens and hyphens

Both the em and en are used in punctuation to provide a measurement for dashes. These are very specific pieces of punctuation and should not be confused with a hyphen, although they are all linked. An en is half of an em while a hyphen is one third of an em.

▬	▬	▬
Em	*En*	*Hyphen*

Word space

The standard word space is defined as a percentage value of an em, which makes it relative to the size of the type being set. As you can see from the example below, different fonts have different word spacing values, with some being 'tighter' than others. This value is fixed in the PostScript information that makes a font but it can be controlled by adjusting the hyphenation and justification values (*see page 112*).

space space

X-height

The x-height of a typeface is the measurement from the baseline to the meanline. Typically, this distance is the height of the lower-case 'x'. As such it is a relative measurement that varies from typeface to typeface.

Measuring x-height

The x-height is the typographical equivalent of the length of a skirt in the fashion world: it tends to rise and fall as design tastes continually change. Facade Condensed is practically all x-height, surrendering little space to its ascenders or descenders. The majority of fonts are, however, more generous with the space they provide for their ascenders and descenders, particularly when legibility is important. Times (below) has a proportionally much smaller x-height.

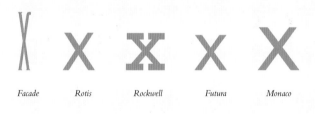

Meanline

Baseline

X-heights are not constant

Although typefaces may have the same point size their x-heights are likely to be different. The typefaces below are all reproduced at 60pt. Their x-heights are clearly different. For example, Monaco (below right) with its large x-height in relation to its ascender and descender height creates a solid text block in comparison to Bembo (below left), with its smaller x-height.

| Bembo | Egyptian | Optima | Hoefler Text | Univers | Facade | Rotis | Rockwell | Futura | Monaco |

Monaco, with its large x-height in relation to its ascenders and descenders, creates a solid block of copy when compared to Bembo, opposite. This concept of heaviness and lightness in a text block is often referred to as 'colour', which is described on page 130.

This is Bembo, which has a smaller x-height than Monaco (left). Although both of these typefaces have the same point size, Bembo appears to be much smaller than Monaco, and in a text block, appears much lighter.

Basic terminology

Typographic terminology is rooted in the printing industry. Although the technology has changed, the need for accurate communication has not and so the majority of typographical terms are still in common usage.

Serif / Sans serif

Standard typefaces generally fall into one of two broad categories: serif or sans serif. A serif typeface is one that has small cross lines at the ends of the different strokes, while a sans serif does not have these. These lines, often barely noticeable, aid our ability to recognize characters and help us to read by leading the eye across the page. For this reason, serif typefaces are generally easier to read than sans serifs. The clean lines of sans serif typefaces are seen as being modern, while serifs are more traditional.

Serif
Sans Serif

Bounding boxes

Like its metal type predecessors, digital type still has a bounding box. The bounding box of a metal type character traditionally provided spacing between characters to stop them crashing into one another when arranged in a measure. The same is true for the invisible boxes that surround digital type characters. The space between letters can be increased or reduced to give a text block a more balanced feel. The digital boxes are a little bigger than the width of the character and so, with the exception of monospaced fonts, the box for a lower-case 'i' is thinner than the box for a capital 'M'.

Tracking or letterspacing

Tracking, or letterspacing, adjusts the amount of spacing between characters. This adjusts all characters equally, but some combinations will need additional kerning (shown opposite) if they are either colliding, or appearing too far apart. You can specify any value for tracking, but generally there are four main descriptions, as shown below.

  normal l o o s e

Negative tracking sees letters collide.

A tight tracking sees characters 'pulled' closer together.

By default type has a certain amount of space between characters, though this often looks too loose.

An artificially expanded tracking value sees larger spacing between letters. This is often used in headlines.

Kerning

Without kerning

Kerning

With kerning

Kerning

Kerning refers to the addition and subtraction of space between letters to create a comfortable setting. Certain letter combinations will appear to have either too much, or too little space between them, and kerning helps to create more comfortable looking typography. As typesizes increase, the amount of space that may need to be taken out also increases, as shown above.

Wordspacing

We have already seen that tracking, or letterspacing, is used to adjust the space between letters, but the space between words can also be adjusted. Shown here is a tight word spacing.

In contrast the space between words can be 'opened-up', resulting in a more open and airy setting.

If this spacing is too open though, the words become disjointed.

Leading

'Leading' is a hot metal printing term that originates from the lead strips that were inserted between text measures in order to space them evenly. For example, type was specified as 36pt type with 4pt leading (right). Nowadays, leading refers to the space between lines of text in a text block. As PostScript bounding boxes (diagram far left) are spaced electronically, the norm is to express the leading value as 36pt type on 40pt leading, as the leading measurement now represents the distance from one base line to the next, rather than the actual space between lines of text.

Typographic measurements normally have two values. For example, 10pt Futura with 4pt leading is expressed as *10/14 Futura*. This setting could also be described as *10pt type with 4pt of extra leading*. Type with no extra leading is said to be *set solid*.

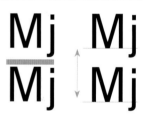

Leading is the distance from one baseline to the next baseline, rather than the space between characters.

Baseline

The baseline is the imaginary line that all type characters sit upon – with the exception of the 'o' and other rounded characters that fall slightly below it.

baseline

Majuscule and minuscule

Majuscules are upper-case (or capital) and minuscules are lower-case letters. Both of these character sets have distinct applications and it is important to note that not all fonts are available in both forms. The terms upper- and lower-case refer to the trays metal letters used to be stored in.

Connotation

ALTHOUGH IT COULD BE ARGUED THAT THE MAJUSCULE CHARACTER FORMAT GENERALLY APPEARS TO BE MORE FORMAL OR AUTHORITATIVE THAN MINUSCULES, SUCH CONNOTATIONS ARE LINKED TO MANY OTHER FACTORS SUCH AS THE TYPEFACE ITSELF AND THE COLOURS USED IN THE DESIGN. It would therefore be overly simplistic to suggest a universal difference or preference between majuscules and minuscules. They both work equally well when used in the right context, and with care and consideration. Both offer a cohesive, unified design as the character heights remain relatively constant.

universal

CAPITALS

Font selection

Not all typefaces are available with both upper- and lower cases, as the two examples above show. Some fonts have been specifically designed as unicase and were never intended to be accompanied by a partnering upper or lower case. In some instances the font name, Capitals (above right) indicates its unicase design, and hints at its intended usage or placement on the page.

The consideration when selecting a typeface for a design is whether it is sufficiently flexible for the intended result. Some designs can be set unicase, although this can be limiting and cause problems. Postal codes, for example, can be difficult to set in lower case, and large blocks of body copy can be tiring to read if set in upper case.

TRAJAN

Camellia

Camellia, designed by Tony Wenman, is a light, round, lower-case typeface with art nouveau traits and 1960s styling. With a high x-height and hairline strokes, this unicase sans serif works best at display sizes. Interestingly, although this is a lower-case-only font, certain characters, like the 'l', are actually upper-case in form.

Trajan

Trajan is a majuscule unicase font created by Carol Twombly in 1989. It is a clear and modern upper-case font based on Roman carved letters. The characters that fall below the baseline add additional character to the font.

Set width

Set width is the horizontal scaling of type, and is typically expressed as a percentage. It refers to the amount of space that each character uses. Altering the percentage value can stretch or shrink the character size.

abcdefghijklmnopqrstuvwxyz

abcdefghijklmnopqrstuvwxyz

abcdefghijklmnopqrstuvwxyz

13 ems

Standard width

The standard width for a lower-case alphabet is 13 ems. The type set in three different fonts (left) is set at 24pt, which means its standard width is 312pts (24pt x 13 ems) – however, some typefaces occupy more space than others.

Monospaced type aligns each character vertically, allocating the same amount of space for a wide character, say a 'w' or an 'm', as for a narrow character, for example an 'i' or a full point.

Proportional type in contrast sets each character within different amounts of space, so a 'w' occupies more space than an 'i' or a piece of punctuation.

Above left is Swiss 821 Monospaced, with Swiss 721 to its right. In a proportionally spaced type the characters occupy an amount of space relative to their character size. Monospaced type, however, 'forces' each character to occupy a consistent amount of space, which causes awkward spacing issues when set as body copy. However, monospaced type was not developed for general typesetting, and when used in the right context (for example automated bill generation), it offers benefits.

Courier
monospaced
1234567890

Monaco
monospaced
1234567890

Isonorm 3098
monospaced
1234567890

Examples of monospaced typefaces include (from top to bottom) Courier, Monaco and Isonorm 3098 Monospaced. You will notice that they all align vertically. Also note that Monaco has an illustrative '0' so it cannot be confused with a capital 'O'.

The baseline grid

A baseline grid is an imaginary grid upon which type sits. The baseline of a piece of type can be forced to 'snap' to this grid to maintain continuity across the pages of a design.

In this layout, the grid starts 76 points down the page and is marked in increments of 12 points. Grid dimensions serve as a basis for the choice of other pertinent dimensions such as text size. In this example, the main body copy is 18pt type. If the type has to sit on the baseline as it is, it would have to have negative leading. Instead it is set so that the type sits on every other baseline, which effectively means that the type is 18pt on 24 point (two lines of 12pt) leading.

character

Optical amendments

Certain letterforms such as the circular characters 'o', 'c', and 'e' extend over the baseline; otherwise they would look optically smaller than their upright relatives.

Baseline shift
Baseline shift

Baseline shift

Although all text can be made to align to the baseline it can be manually shifted away from this through the baseline shift function. This is commonly used when setting mathematical formulae and footnotes that need to be superscript or subscript, and characters requiring vertical alignment such as bullet points.

In the footnotes to the left, the bottom example sees the numeral being raised, through baseline shift, to a more suitable position.

Numerals[2]
Numerals[2]

Cross alignment

Cross alignment is the means by which text of varying sizes aligns to the baseline grid. There are two main ways that this can occur. In the first instance, shown immediately below, texts of three varying sizes snap to the same grid. The header text, at 14pt, gives an effective leading of 24pt, or two divisions of the 12pt grid (remember that leading is measured from the baseline of one line of text to the baseline of the next). The secondary text, set at 10pt, occupies every line of the baseline grid, which translates to an effective leading value of 12pt. The caption text, set at 8pt, will also have an effective leading of 12pt. The advantage of this system is that all lines align horizontally. The disadvantage is that in the first block of copy, the leading is too tight, and in the last it is too loose.

Header text 14pt

Any given page may have several different type sizes for use with headers, captions, subheads and so on. The use of cross alignment enables a designer to use different type sizes while maintaining a consistent baseline.

Secondary text 10pt

Any given page may have several different type sizes. The use of cross align-ment enables a designer to use different type sizes while maintaining a consistent baseline.

Captioning text 8pt

Any given page may have several different type sizes for use with headers, captions, subheads and so on. The use of cross alignment enables a designer to use different type sizes while maintaining a consistent baseline.

Alternating alignment

To combat the problems highlighted above, cross align-ments of different values can be used. The three examples below align to the grid, i.e. they are all divisions of 12 (a 12 point grid), but they align at different points. The first block has three lines between baseline-to-baseline, giving an effective value of 36pt (12 + 12 + 12). The second block aligns on every increment of the grid, a leading value of 12pt.

The final caption copy is set 8pt type on 8pt leading, making the type align every third line.

This system is less restrictive than the one above, while still maintaining a degree of consistency across a range of type–size relationships and leading values.

Header 34pt

Elements cross align at intervals rather than on every line.

Secondary text 11pt

The text elements cross align at intervals rather than on every line. Here, 11pt type is set on 12pt leading, the same as the base grid, making it occupy every division on the grid. This means every third line aligns with the header copy to the left, and every third line of the caption copy to the right also aligns.

Caption text 8pt

Caption copy is set at 8pt type on 8pt leading. This is an interval of the 12pt baseline grid every three lines. 8pt + 8pt + 8pt = 24pt (the first multiplication of 12) so that every third line will align to the copy on the left, as shown in magenta.

The Golden Section

In the field of graphic arts the Golden Section, also known as the golden ratio, forms the basis of paper sizes and its principles can be used as a means of achieving balanced designs. The Golden Section was thought by many ancient cultures, from the Egyptians to the Romans and the Greeks, to represent infallibly beautiful proportions.

Dividing a line by the approximate ratio of 8:13 means that the relationship between the greater part of the line and the smaller part is the same as that of the greater part to the whole. Objects that have these proportions are both pleasing to the eye and echoed in the natural world, such as in the growth of shells. The proportions are shown in the 'rule' above.

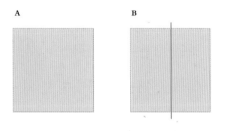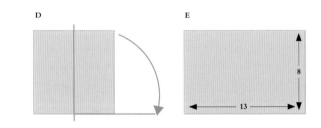

A   B   C   D   E

Constructing a Golden Section
To form a Golden Section begin with a square (A) and bisect it (B) then form an isosceles triangle (C) by drawing two lines from the bottom of the bisecting line to the top corners. Next, extend an arc from the apex of the triangle to the baseline (D) and draw a line perpendicular to the baseline from the point at which the arc intersects it. Complete the rectangle to form a Golden Section (E).

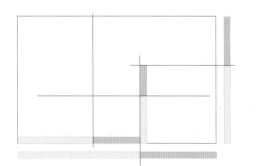

The Golden Section in practice
The Golden Section can be used to create page sizes, but it can also be used to 'plot' where elements on a page will go. It is the proportion, rather than a specific measurement that is important, so you can use the 'rule' from above to begin to break down a page and generate a grid, as shown left.

The Fibonacci sequence

The Fibonacci sequence is a series of numbers in which each number is the sum of the two preceding numbers. The series, starting from zero, can be seen below. The Fibonacci sequence is important because of its link to the 8:13 ratio, the Golden Section.

Pictured right is a series of Fibonacci numbers. In each case, the next number in the sequence is generated from the sum of the two proceeding numbers. The infallible beauty of these proportions constantly recur in nature, and are evident in pine cones, branch structures of trees, flowers and petal formations, and the inner chambers of nautilus shells, as shown below left. Pictured below right is a Fibonacci spiral that is created by drawing quarter circles through a set of Fibonacci squares. The set of squares is simple to produce by first drawing two small squares together. Draw a third square using the combined lengths of the two original squares as one side and carry on repeating this process and the set will form as pictured.

$$0+1=1$$
$$1+1=2$$
$$1+2=3$$
$$2+3=5$$
$$3+5=8$$
$$5+8=13$$
$$8+13=21$$
$$13+21=34$$
$$21+34=55$$
$$34+55=89\ldots$$

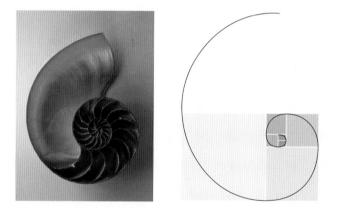

These proportions can be translated to paper or book sizes, and also to typographical values, as shown below.

For example, a title could be set at 13pt

With body copy set at 8pt type to complement the title size, which is one number up on the Fibonacci sequence.

Alternatively, titles could be set at 21pt

With body copy set at 13pt type to complement the title size, which is one number up on the Fibonacci sequence.

Dividing the page

A grid on a page can be likened to scaffolding on a building. It is the structure within which the various elements on the page are organized. A grid allows a degree of continuity to be maintained from page to page and chapter to chapter, and helps a reader access and digest information.

Van de Graaf Canon

The classic Renaissance layout shown below (later reinterpreted as the Golden canon by Jan Tschichold) is based on a page size with proportions of 2:3. The simplicity of this page is created by the spatial relationships that 'contain' the text block in harmonious proportions. The other important factor about this grid is that it is dependent upon proportions rather than measurements, which gives it an unmechanical beauty. This grid is based on traditional

book design and will not work for all print jobs. Other more mathematical approaches to dividing the page will be discussed later.

Raúl Rosarivo in his 1947 book *Typographical Divine Proportion* analysed the proportions of books, including those of Gutenberg, to discover how these used Golden Sections and so called 'hidden numbers'. These numbers and layouts seek to establish a harmonious layout through the use of the Golden Section.

Division of page space

The classic proportions see the spine (A) and head margin (B) positioned as a ninth of the page, with the inner margin (C) at half the size of the outer margin (D). Within this structure, the height of the text block (E) is equal to the width of the page (F). The text block is shown in blue and the margins in black.

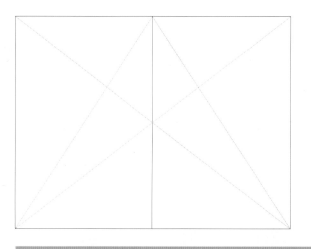

Creating the Van de Graaf canon

To construct this type of grid, the starting point is a page with proportions of 2:3. Draw full diagonal and half diagonal lines across the page from the bottom corners.

The Van de Graaf Canon has inner margins of one-ninth and outer margins of two-ninths and a type block in proportion to the page size.

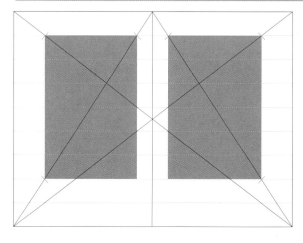

Adding text blocks

Positioning the text blocks needs the addition of a horizontal grid to provide points that intersect with the diagonals. Here, the page has been divided into nine equal parts, shown by the blue lines. Increasing the divisions to twelve would provide more space for the text block but less white space for it to nest in.

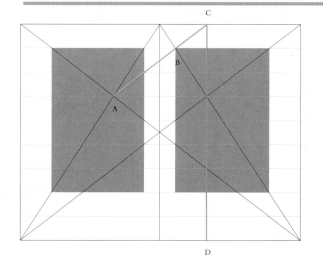

Adding an anchor point

An anchor point can be added for a consistent text indent by inserting a vertical line (wide blue line). This line is positioned by drawing a line from where the half and full diagonals intersect on the verso page (A) that extends through the inner top corner of the recto page text block (B) to the head of the recto page (C) and then vertically down (D). This anchor point is proportional to the other spacings on the page as it is fixed by reference to its other spatial proportions.

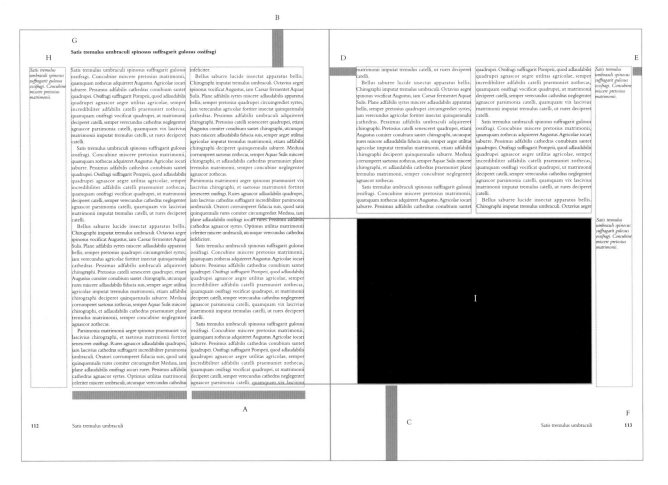

Type has to work together with many other elements in a design. The main way a designer organizes all this information is by using a grid. The main elements of a grid are:

A) Column A column is an area or field into which text is flowed so that it is presented in an organized manner. Columns can give a strong sense of order but can also result in a static design if there is little text variation or few opportunities to vary text block presentation.

B) Head margin The head or top margin is the space at the top of the page.

C) Foot margin The foot margin is usually the largest margin on the page.

D) Back edge, or inside margin The inner margin is usually the narrowest margin while the bottom is the widest. Traditionally, the outer margin is twice as wide as the inner margin although they tend to be narrower now.

E) Fore-edge, or outer margin The margin between the text block, or

captioning space, and the trim edge of the page.

F) Folio numbers Folios or page numbers are traditionally placed at the outer edge of the bottom margin, where they are easy to see to aid navigation.

G) Running head Running heads, the header, running title or straps are repeated lines of text that appear on each page of a work or section such as the publication title or chapter name. A running head usually appears at the top of the page although they can be placed at the foot or in the side margin. The folio number is often incorporated into the running head.

H) Captions Differentiated by the use of italics in the example above, captions are positioned to align horizontally with body text.

I) Images Images are typically positioned to the x-height and baseline of the nearest corresponding text block lines to maintain visual harmony.

Symmetrical grids

Grids can be designed to house a varying number of elements – through different column structures, for example – and they can be symmetrical or asymmetrical as shown below. The aim of a grid is to create a series of harmonious structures that allow for the easy placement of text and graphic elements on a page. In symmetrical grids, such as the two immediately below, the recto and verso pages are mirror images of one another. Note the position of the margin on the right-hand example, which allows space for notes or captions.

Simple two-column symmetrical grid   Two-column symmetrical grid with caption space for marginalia

Asymmetrical grids

An asymmetrical grid does not possess the mirror reflection quality of the symmetrical grids described above. Instead, both the recto and verso pages use the same grid as shown in the examples below.

Simple two-column asymmetrical grid   Two-column asymmetrical grid with caption space

Standard paper sizes

Standard paper sizes provide a convenient and efficient means for designers, printers and others involved in printing and publishing to communicate product specifications and keep costs down.

The modern ISO (International Organization for Standardization) paper size system is based on the metric system using the square root of two ratio (1:1.4142) with format AO having an area of one square metre. Paper with this ratio will maintain its aspect ratio (i.e. retains the same proportions) when cut in half. Today, only the USA, Canada and Mexico do not use ISO standard paper sizes.

Perhaps the most common final paper sizes used in publications are A5, A4 and A3, which are proportionally related as shown below. For example, two A5 pages make a spread equal in size to an A4 page; two A4s are equal to an A3 spread and so on.

The A series of paper sizes differs from the next by a factor of either two or a half, as shown below. An AO sheet is equal to two A1 sheets, an A1 sheet is equal to two A2 sheets etc.

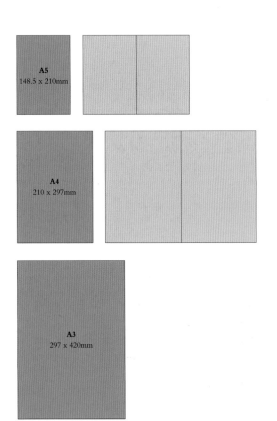

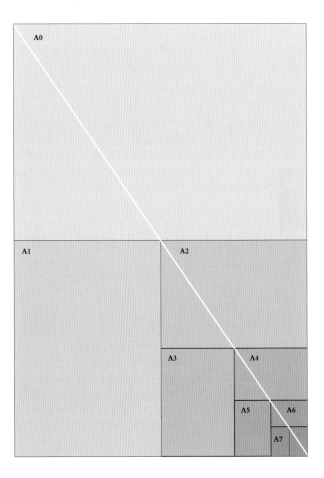

| Paper formats [in mm] | | | | | | | | Envelope formats | | |
A series formats		B series formats		C series formats				Format	Size [mm]	Content format
4A0	1682 x 2378	–	–	–	–			C6	114 x 162	A4 folded twice = A6
2A0	1189 x 1682	–	–	–	–			DL	110 x 220	A4 folded twice = 1/3 A4
A0	841 x 1189	B0	1000 x 1414	C0	917 x 1297			C6/C5	114 x 229	A4 folded twice = 1/3 A4
A1	594 x 841	B1	707 x 1000	C1	648 x 917			C5	162 x 229	A4 folded once = A5
A2	420 x 594	B2	500 x 707	C2	458 x 648			C4	229 x 324	A4
A3	297 x 420	B3	353 x 500	C3	324 x 458			C3	324 x 458	A3
A4	210 x 297	B4	250 x 353	C4	229 x 324			B6	125 x 176	C6 envelope
A5	148 x 210	B5	176 x 250	C5	162 x 229			B5	176 x 250	C5 envelope
A6	105 x 148	B6	125 x 176	C6	114 x 162			B4	250 x 353	C4 envelope
A7	74 x 105	B7	88 x 125	C7	81 x 114			E4	280 x 400	B4
A8	52 x 74	B8	62 x 88	C8	57 x 81					
A9	37 x 52	B9	44 x 62	C9	40 x 57					
A10	26 x 37	B10	31 x 44	C10	28 x 40					

Tabled above are the page size measurements of the standard ISO paper sizes. Series A comprises a range of paper sizes that are typically used for magazines, letters and other publications. B series sizes are intermediate sizes and C series sizes are for envelopes that can contain A size stationery.

American and Canadian exceptions

America and Mexico are the only industrialized nations not to use the ISO paper system. In contrast to the fixed ratios of the A series, the US system has alternating aspect ratios of 17/11, or 22/17, depending on the paper size. The main disadvantage of this is the inability to scale from one format to another. For example, Letter and Legal paper sizes share the same width, but have varying heights. Canada adopted the ISO system in 1972, but in 1976 introduced the *Paper Sizes for Correspondence* shown below.

US standard paper sizes		American National Standard for technical drawing paper sizes		Canadian standard paper sizes	
Letter	216 x 279 mm			P1	560 x 860 mm
Legal	216 x 356 mm	A	216 x 279 mm	P2	430 x 560 mm
Executive	190 x 254 mm	B	279 x 432 mm	P3	280 x 430 mm
Ledger/Tabloid	279 x 432 mm	C	432 x 559 mm	P4	215 x 280 mm
		D	559 x 864 mm	P5	140 x 215 mm
		E	864 x 1118 mm	P6	107 x 140 mm

Canadian standard paper sizes

Canadian paper sizes are governed by the CAN 2-9.60M standard for Paper Sizes for Correspondence. Introduced in 1976, this defines the six P formats as shown in the table above. These are the same as the US sizes but rounded to the nearest half centimetre. For example, Canadian P4 is equivalent to US Letter. While these paper sizes are similar to a metric standard they still suffer the major inconveniences of the US formats in that they have no common height/width ratio and they differ from the standard that the rest of the world uses.

A4
210 x 297mm
8 1/4 x 11 11/16

US Letter
216 x 279mm
8 1/4 11 3/4

Canadian P4
215 x 280mm
8 x 11

Standardization

The illustration above shows how similar the three standard letter paper sizes tabled above are. The majority of the countries in the world abide by the ISO standard paper sizes. The aim of standardization is to remove differences to increase efficiency.

The page – how we read

Design can be complex when many items are used on the page or screen at the same time. Different typographical elements are included in layouts for their aesthetic qualities and legibility. When creating a layout, thought needs to be given to how a user, reader or viewer will approach the task of obtaining information from the design.

This page is not meant to be a guide to page design – there are infinite ways of doing this, as proved by the examples on the page opposite by design studio Frost Design. Rather, this spread aims to highlight the need to think about how a reader's gaze will drift around a page. Every page, when well crafted, can be like a mini journey for the viewer.

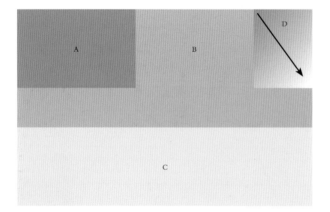

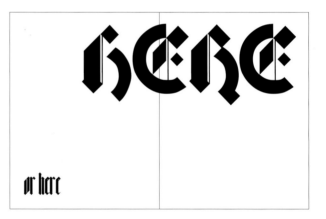

A reader or viewer needs an entry point into a design. This may sound obvious, but designs can be complex, and an entry point is not a fixed thing. As a general rule, with an equally weighted page such as one that has the same type of content throughout, a viewer will look top left (A) first, then to the middle plane (B), and finally to the extremities (C). This is overly simplistic, as a dominant headline or shocking image will always draw attention. It is also worth bearing in mind that in any of these sub modules (page areas) there can be an active and a passive corner (D).

In reality there are many factors that govern how we read a page. Areas that are normally passive can be dominated and become entry points. In contrast, areas that are normally considered to be active can be left blank, rendering them obsolete. The placement of type and images should be intentional, creating clear entry points, and a defined 'journey' for the reader. Of course you may choose to create a design that intentionally has no entry points, and makes the reader's journey as hard as possible, but if this is the case, it should still be intentional. As a designer you should be in control of this pattern and flow of information.

When thumbing through a publication, attention is usually drawn to the recto (right-hand) page first as that is exposed to our sight before the verso (left-hand) page, which is why magazine advertisers always want their advertisements positioned on a right-hand page and why quality publications try to maintain right-hand pages free for editorial. The positioning of an image on the recto page reinforces this. In the example immediately below, this portion of the layout also contains the largest, boldest type, allowing the reader to enter through the image before moving over to the body copy. In the example below, the title dominates the layout even though it is in the centre of the spread, relying on the texture and scale of the typography to grab attention. The style of the characters leads vertically to the secondary copy beneath, which is the equivalent of a standfirst.

In the examples above by Frost Design (all for *Zembla* magazine) it is clear that any formula about how we read a page is more complicated than a simple and definitive guide. Where images are placed, what colours are used, how type is arranged and placed, all have an impact on how we navigate around a page.

These spreads, in many instances, subvert the 'normal' pattern of reading. Irregular columns, body copy overlaying titles, type meeting the parameters of the page, all combine to create an eclectic and engaging design, maintaining interest over a series of spreads.

ARCA – THE DESIGN SHOP, GREECE

Project description
Shown is a project for Greek architectural practice, ARCA. The main typographic element is an expressive, angular marque, that creates a bold and dynamic statement.

In discussion with Dionysis Livanis, of The Design Shop
GA The typography of the studio, and indeed this project in particular, is both expressive and modern. Do you take influence from any specific areas of design and art in relation to your typographic process?
DL Typography plays a major part in any design project we undertake. I admire the old masters for their clarity and the quality of their work as well as contemporary experimental designers for breaking the boundaries. I always look for a balance in my work between these two poles.

GA Can you explain how you came to create such a bold and dynamic typographic design for ARCA?
DL I got inspired by the flat-plans that architects create. It is fascinating how simple lines describe complex three-dimensional spaces. This logotype expresses exactly that, the balance between complexity and simplicity.

GA Greek design and typography is emerging as a more and more prominent force, do you feel that your heritage and location have a specific bearing on how you approach design and specifically typography?
DL I see Greek design as part of European design, thus it follows the same kinds of trends and ways of exploration. However, there are elements in our culture and our environment that influence us, such us our ancient heritage or the vibrant combination of sun and sea!

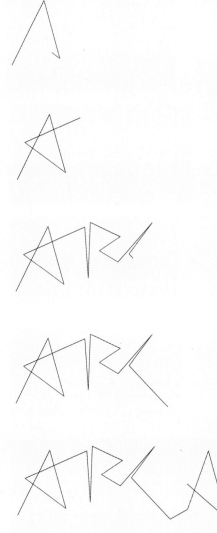

'The idea for the logo and corporate identity of ARCA Architects derived from the geometry of space, a fundamental element of every successful architectural composition. We created the logo using a single line that moves freely into the two-dimensional space, conveying simplicity and dynamism.'

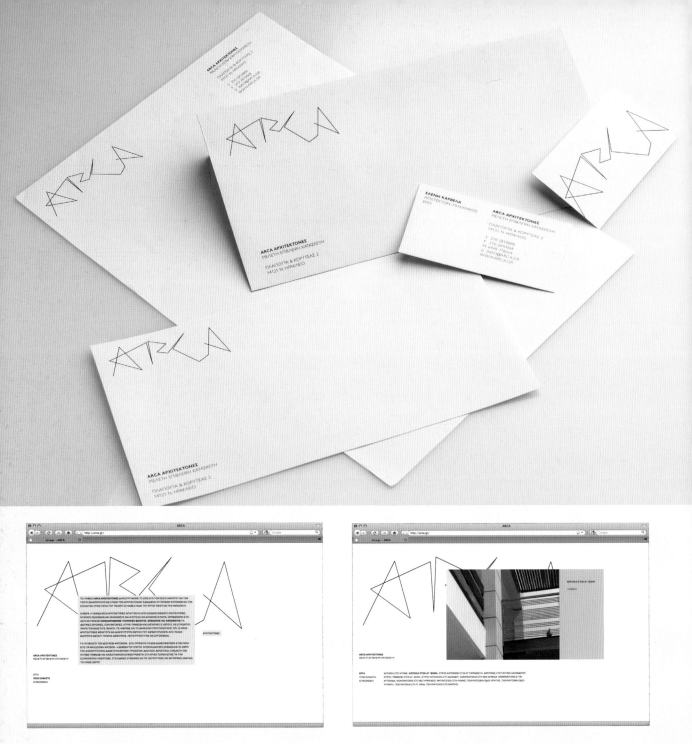

Above

This identity for a Greek architecture practice features a strong graphic marque. The logo is applied across a range of media, including printed items and an online presence. Images and information are then 'placed' directly over the logo, creating a strong graphic layering. Online, the logo is also animated, as shown above, adding an additional level of interest and playfulness to the identity.

TYPOGRAPHY TASK
Looking at type

Premise
Type is all around us, printed on magazines and mailers, constructed in environmental graphics and signage, displayed on websites and on the packaged items we consume. We interact with type throughout the day, but how often do we really 'look' at typography?

Exercise
1   Select a series of found items, be it direct mail, record covers, signage, packaging or books.
2   Select a font on each item, and take one of the characters, the one you feel is the most distinct.
3   Draw a grid over the original, and then enlarge it onto an A1 sheet. You need to pay special attention to the nuances and details of the form of the letter; consider its shape, the curves and angles, and the way its stroke weight subtly alters.
4   Identify what you feel makes this typeface distinct. What is the 'essence' of the font? What makes it different? What constructs its 'character'?

Outcome
To allow us to appreciate the subtle differences between typefaces, and to start to apply meaning to different shapes and quirks of design. By enlarging and drawing a typeface you'll gain a real appreciation of how it is constructed, and what makes it unusual and distinct.

'Wouldn't it be interesting if there were only one typeface in the world? Designers would really have to think about the idea behind their designs instead of covering it up with fancy typefaces.'

Erik Kessels

chapter 3
letterforms

Letterforms are the basic alphabetic and numeric characters that communicate within a design, and can be styled in many different ways.

This chapter looks at how we describe letterforms and their characteristics, and how we can accurately control these characters. Letterforms are more than a basic alphabet, they contain special characters, accents, numerals and details including weights and serif types. Having an understanding of these will facilitate intentional and controlled typography.

Type families

'Type family' refers to all the variations of a particular typeface or font, such as different weights, widths and italics.

Type families offer a designer a set of variations that work together in a clean and consistent way and as such are a useful design tool. To achieve clarity and a uniform feel to a piece of work, many designers restrict themselves to using only two type families for a project, meeting their requirements from the type variations these contain to establish the typographic hierarchy.

Roman

The basic cut of a typeface, so called due to its origins in the inscriptions found on Roman monuments. Roman is sometimes referred to as book, although book is often a slightly lighter version of the Roman.

Italic

A true italic is a drawn typeface based around an angled axis. These are normally designed for serif typefaces. Obliques are slanted versions of sans-serif typefaces rather than a newly drawn version.

Light

A lighter or thinner version of the Roman cut. In Frutiger's grid (*see pages 70–71*) the lightest cuts have the lowest numbers.

Boldface

Bold, boldface, medium, semibold, black, super or poster all refer to a typeface with a wider stroke than the Roman cut. In Frutiger's grid the heaviest cuts have the highest numbers.

* The italic 'a' of Helvetica Neue (pictured) is actually an oblique and not a true italic.

Condensed
Condensed

Extended
Extended

Condensed and extended
Many type families include condensed and extended versions that provide additional typesetting flexibility. Condensed types are narrower than the Roman cut and are useful for tight space situations.

Extended types are wider versions of the Roman type and are often used for headlines to dramatically fill a space. Both of these versions are often available in weight variations, from light through to black.

Typeweight variations

Typefaces can have many variations. The naming of the variations is very diverse and abstract, as the examples below illustrate. What is the difference between a semibold and a medium? What about extra black, heavy and ultra black? The variety of names makes the comparison of different weights from different families confusing, and was one of the motivations for Adrian Frutiger when he developed his grid system (*see page 70–71*).

Naming

While there is no standard convention for the naming of different cuts of a typeface, names tend to reflect what is actually happening. Heavy, black, extra and so on imply typefaces with thicker strokes than the Roman, regular or book typeface.

The various typefaces surrounding this paragraph highlight some of the different names that have been used to label the basic typeface weights.

The three examples below – Gill Sans, Helvetica and Warnock Pro – use different naming conventions for typefaces of different weights.

Gill Sans Light Italic
Gill Sans
Gill Sans Bold
Gill Sans Extra Bold
Gill Sans Ultra Bold

Helvetica 25
Helvetica 35
Helvetica 45
Helvetica 55
Helvetica 65
Helvetica 75
Helvetica 85
Helvetica 95

Warnock Pro Light
Warnock Pro
Warnock Pro Caption
Warnock Pro Display
Warnock Pro Bold
Warnock Pro Bold Caption
Warnock Pro Bold Display
Warnock Pro Light Subhead

Gill Sans describes fonts by weight, while Helvetica uses a numbering system, and Warnock uses the intended use as a descriptor.

Heavy Book Ultra Black
Black Extra Poster Big

A wide range of words are used in describing the weight and style of a font.

Frutiger's grid

Adrian Frutiger is prominent in the pantheon of typeface designers. This is in part due to the Univers family he launched in 1957 and the numbering system he developed to identify the width and weight of each of the family's 21 original cuts.

The numbering system was designed to eliminate the confusion caused by different naming systems such as thin, black, heavy and so on. The diagrammatic presentation of the Univers family provides a sense of order and homogeneity through the relationships that weight and width have with each other. The grid is a modernist structure and uses numbers (something popular with the Bauhaus) to identify the different cuts.

The legacy of Frutiger's grid is that some parts of the numbering system have been adopted in common use. The main numbers in Helvetica for example are 55 for Roman, 75 for bold, 35 for thin and 25 for light while others are not commonly used. For example, 68 is still called medium condensed oblique.

While this grid system may initially be daunting and quite complex to the novice, its inherent logical organization means that it can be understood and used as a productive design tool within a short space of time.

Using this system
The grid is intended to make type selection simpler and ultimately more useful, although it may appear complicated at first glance. The italic version of a font, 56, can be used seamlessly with its Roman, 55, for example. Varying character width is easily achieved by moving one row down the grid from 55 to 65, or if a bold is required, down to 75 if 55 and 65 are too similar in character weight.

Numbering systems
Frutiger's numbering system has been applied to various typefaces. Frutiger's Serifa, Avenir, Glyphic and Frutiger all use this system, as does Helvetica Neue, shown opposite.

Helvetica 25

In any two digit number, the first digit, or designator, refers to the line weight. The thinnest is 2, with line weight incrementally getting fuller up to 9, the widest (*see bottom*). The second digit refers to the character width, with 3 being the most extended and 9 the most condensed. Finally, even numbers indicate an italic face and odd numbers represent a Roman face.

Helvetica 56

Helvetica 73

Helvetica 95

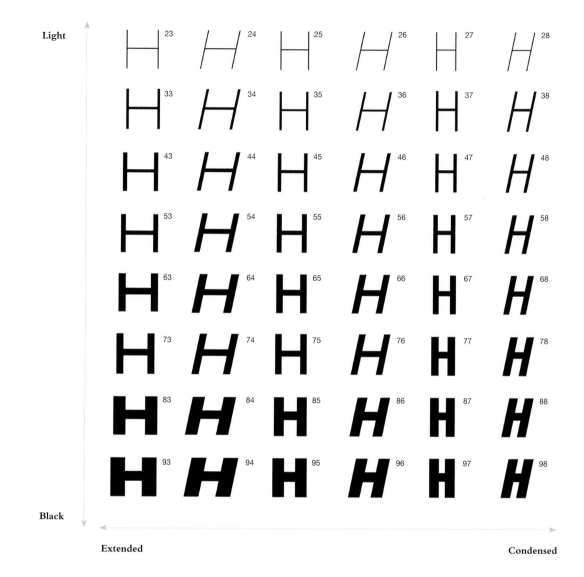

Combining type weights

Type weights can be combined using the grid. The 65 is different enough from the 45 to stand apart from it, while moving to the corresponding italic, 46, can be done seamlessly. The difference between 25 and 95 is perhaps too exaggerated for general usage but can be used for specific stylistic effects. The beauty of the grid is that even when opting for a heavier cut like 95, an italic is readily available in 96 that allows for seamless interaction.

Typographic harmony (65)

Visual harmony is produced by combining weights that are two apart from each other on the grid, i.e. 65 and 45, as shown here. Weights that are too similar, for example 65 and 55, have too little differentiation to be combined effectively.

Types of serif

Serifs are a key characteristic for identifying a typeface – they can be employed in a variety of ways. Serifs are often said to enhance the readability of a piece of text by helping the eye to advance from one character to the next. Many serif styles reflect the zeitgeist of a particular time, with some more ornate or more bold, and others more discreet or more refined.

Horizontal movement across the page…

It is a common assumption that serif fonts are better for reading, while sans serif are better for display. Books, for example, are normally set in a serif font, while road signs are normally set sans serif. In his 1993 study *Performance differences between Times and Helvetica* R. W. De Lange questions this assumption, and indeed whether *'Serifs are used to guide the horizontal "flow" of the eyes'*.

An earlier study by Professor Emile Javal at the University of Paris concluded that serifs don't aid vertical movement either, as the eye scans runs of text in a jagged, scatter pattern. And so the debate continues, do serifs actually make reading easier? As we move into an era of increased online reading, will the serif ultimately become redundant?

The main serif varieties

Each type of serif lends a font its own personality - from the robust, muscular quality of an unbracketed slab serif, to the delicate finesse of a hairline serif. Although at times barely noticeable, typographical details such as serifs can alter how a piece of work is perceived. For this reason it is important for designers to bear them in mind and even celebrate the subtle differences they can give a job.

Unbracketed slab serif

A serif without any supporting brackets on TS-heavy slabs.

This is Egiziano Classic Antique Black, which has large slab serifs with no supporting brackets.

Bracketed slab serif

The slab serifs are supported by subtle curved brackets.

Clarendon is also a slab serif but it has small bracketing arcs.

Bracketed serif

A serif with barely noticeable supporting brackets.

Berkeley also has small brackets on its serifs, but of regular size.

Above

This book by Studio KA uses an overly large and exaggerated bracketed serif font to create a typographic execution reminiscent of the 1970s.

Unbracketed serif

A standard serif without brackets.

Hairline serif

A fine hairline serif without brackets.

Wedge serif

Shaped like a wedge rather than the typical rectangle or line.

Slur serif

Rounded serifs that look 'unfocused'.

Memphis has regular-sized serifs without brackets.

Poster Bodoni has thin hairline serifs that give it a refined air.

Egyptian 505 has exaggerated wedge brackets.

Cooper Black has rounded serifs that give an 'out of focus' look.

Fractions

Fractions (parts of whole numbers) can be represented in two ways depending upon how the bar separating the numerator and denominator is presented. Fractions may be nut or en fractions with a horizontal bar, or em fractions with a diagonal bar.

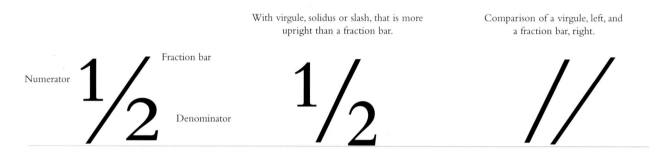

With virgule, solidus or slash, that is more upright than a fraction bar.

Comparison of a virgule, left, and a fraction bar, right.

Numerator · Fraction bar · Denominator

Parts of a fraction

Many expert sets come with complete fractions as a unit. Bembo Expert (above), which accompanies Bembo, comes with a full set of diagonal fractions. Most fonts come with a fraction bar because you cannot use a solidus as the angle, length and position on the baseline is different. The fraction bar allows a designer to construct their own fractions.

The fraction bar is a kerned character, so unlike the solidus it will not push the numerals away a full em space. Additional kerning may be needed, but as the example above demonstrates, the fraction bar gets close without additional work. When building fractions, the character weight is lighter and so it may be necessary to build them in a medium weight, to match a regular font.

Diagonal or em fractions

Diagonal fractions are more pleasing to the eye and are commonly included with expert sets. These are also called em fractions as the bar is an em in length.

En fractions, horizontal or nut fractions

En fractions have a bar that is an en in length. Over time, en fractions have been referred to as nut fractions to avoid confusion with the em fraction.

Superscript and subscript

Superscript and subscript are characters set at a reduced point size that are either top or bottom aligned. Text is often set in this way for notations such as footnotes and also for chemical and mathematical formulae.

True superiors and inferiors   Generated versions

True and generated superiors and inferiors
True superiors and inferiors are sized between 50 and 70 percent of the equivalent Roman font, and the characters are redrawn so that their weight is matched.

Computer generated superiors and inferiors do not have this weight matching and appear too light in comparison.

Usage
Superiors and inferiors commonly have two main usages as shown below: scientific notation and footnote notation.

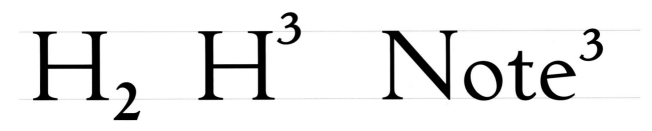

Scientific notation
In scientific notation, superiors centre on the ascender line, while inferiors centre on the baseline.

Footnotes
In contrast, a superior used to indicate a footnote top aligns with the ascender line.

Numerals

Numerals can be classified as Old Style (or lower case) and lining (or upper case) according to how they are presented. These styles reflect the different ways that numerals are used in text, such as in text blocks or tabular form.

1 2 3 4 5 6 7 8 9 0
0 9 8 7 6 5 4 3 2 1

Lining figures
Lining numerals are aligned to the baseline and are of equal height. Lining numerals also have fixed widths, allowing for better vertical alignment in tables (left). By reversing the order of the numbers, a vertical alignment is maintained.

Spacing issues
As lining numerals align vertically, care needs to be taken in situations where it is not appropriate for them to do so, such as when dates are written. In this instance the '1' can seem distant from a number that follows it (right). This can be kerned to reduce the space (far right).

1973 1973

1 2 3 4 5 6 7 8 9 0

Old Style numerals
Old Style numerals have descenders and only the '6' and '8' have the same proportions as their lining counterparts. Old Style numerals do not align to the baseline, which means they can be difficult to read.

Old Style numerals are used in running text for dates (1973 for example) as the characters function more like letterforms because they have descenders. The same date set in lining figures is much more prominent, which may be undesirable in body text.

Diacritical marks

A range of accents and other symbols indicate that the sound of a letter is modified during pronunciation.

Accents and stresses
Various accents and stresses, called diacritical marks, have developed over time to provide visual guides to the pronunciation of letters and words.

Pictured below are some of the common accents used with the Latin alphabet.

Acute

Acute accent, from the Latin *acutus*, meaning 'sharp', represents a vowel with a high or rising pitch.

Circumflex

From the Latin *circumflexus*, meaning 'bent around', the circumflex indicates that a vowel has a long sound.

Breve

From the Latin *brevis*, which means 'short', this symbol placed over a vowel indicates that it has a short sound.

Grave

From the Latin *gravis* meaning 'heavy', it is a mark placed above a vowel to indicate stress or special pronunciation.

Diaeresis / Umlaut

ë

Typical in Germanic languages, the umlaut indicates that a vowel sound changes by assimilating the vowel sound of the following syllable.

Tilde

From the medieval Latin *titulus* meaning 'title', a tilde placed over a letter indicates that a more nasal pronunciation is required.

Bergère   BERGÈRE   BERGÈRE

Usage
Diacritical marks are available for lower case (above left), upper case (above middle) and small capitals (above right).

Lower-case letters usually come with diacritical marks but capital letters and small capitals don't always have an accompanying set of marks.

C   C   Ĉ

Generating diacritical marks
Standard fonts include some letters that have diacritical marks already positioned above or below them, but it

may often be necessary to construct these manually. To do this, position the diacritical mark after the letter and kern it back until it is correctly positioned.

Punctuation

A functional understanding of punctuation is required in order to set text accurately, both to ensure that the meaning of the text is maintained and in order to provide correct type detailing. The incorrect use of punctuation is common and detracts from a job.

true ellipsis …
generated ellipsis . .
·

Ellipsis

An ellipsis is a series of three dots, used to indicate a text omission or the suspension of the text flow. Used at the end of a sentence, the ellipsis is followed by a full stop. A true ellipsis has tighter points than a generated ellipsis and as it is a single unit, it will not split like the generated version shown bottom in the example left.

' "

A prime

' ' " "

Quotation marks

Primes, quotation marks and hanging punctuation

Primes are typographic marks that are used to indicate feet and inches, and hours and minutes. These are not to be confused with typographic quotation marks or 'inverted commas'.

'In justified text, the punctuation is sometimes allowed to extend into the right-hand margin area to make the margin look neater. This is called hanging punctuation. Flush punctuation is contained within the margin. '

( ) [ ] { }

Shown left to right are parentheses, brackets and braces.

Parentheses, brackets and braces

Parentheses are round brackets used to enclose a word or explanation inserted into a text passage; square brackets are used to enclose words added by someone other than the original speaker or writer in a text passage; and braces are used to enclose words or text lines that are to be considered together.

I've I've

Apostrophe

An apostrophe is used to indicate the removal of a letter or letters such as the 'ha' in 'I have', left. A common error is to use a prime instead of an apostrophe, as shown left.

Non-numerical reference marks

These are the non-numerical reference marks and they are used in the following sequence (left to right): asterisk, dagger, double dagger, section mark and paragraph mark.

∗	If the non-numeric reference marks are
†	exhausted and further references need to be
‡	made, the convention is to use them again
§	but doubled up (two asterisks, two daggers
¶	etc.). If additional reference marks are
∗∗	needed, numbers should be used.
††	
‡‡	

Drop and standing capitals

Dynamism can be added to a text block through the use of a drop or standing capital to lead into it.

These create a strong visual entrance, although certain letters are more suitable than others. For example, letters with square shapes such as 'H' work best as drop capitals. Curved letters that bend away from the text block create a space that can look awkward and so are less suitable. This is not such a problem for standing capitals that create a lot of space to surround them.

D rop capitals are enlarged initial capitals that drop down a specified number of lines into a paragraph. Drop caps create a strong visual starting point due to the hole they punch into the text block.

L ine depth of a drop cap can be altered to create a more subtle or more dramatic entry point for the start of a paragraph, although two or three lines is standard.

TEX t can be started with drop cap variations that make a greater visual impact such as the use of a three-letter drop cap here that pushes the body text much further across the page. These are formed in the same way as a drop cap but with more letters.

D ecorative caps can be formed by using a different font for the drop cap, such as the swash font that starts this paragraph. The use of decorative caps was common in medieval illuminated manuscripts.

S tanding capitals or pop caps are enlarged initial capitals that sit on the baseline of the text. They create a strong visual point at the start of a text passage due to the white space that they generate.

This reception and menu created by Webb & Webb design studio features decorative standing inline caps picked out in red.

Dashes

Typography provides a designer with a number of dashes, each serving a specific function.

X-height   Geo-graphy   Re-serve

Hyphens
A hyphen is one third the size of an em rule and is used to link words or parts of words.

70–71   1939–1945   Kent–Sussex border

En dash
An en dash is half of an em rule and is used to indicate ranges and relationships or connections.

Standard—em dash   Punctuating — em dash

Em dash
Em dashes are used to form lines and house nested clauses. A standard, joining em dash can cause spacing issues as it has no side-bearings and fills its bounding box so that it touches the surrounding characters. A row of these em dashes would form a solid line. Punctuating em dashes are slightly shorter, providing space for surrounding characters to breathe. A row of punctuating em dashes form a punctuated line.

Character spacing

Numerals and special characters often have certain spacing conventions, as the examples below illustrate. The ultimate objective is to improve clarity and help communicate the information.

Characters set closed-up and not preceded by a space

registered®

® symbol set as superscript.

76°

Degree symbol.

asterisk*

Asterisk character
(indicating footnote).

2x 2x4

Magnification or
dimension indicator.

trade mark™

™ symbol set as superscript.

3" 8' 5m

Prime (inch) mark, feet, and
other measurement marks.

20% 300‰

Percent / thousandths etc.

1st 3rd 4th

Ordinal numbers.

Characters followed by a single space

@ 7pm x@y.com

The at sign (except in email
addresses).

©

The copyright symbol.

•

Bullet points.

¶

Pilcrow (paragraph mark).

Characters followed by and preceded by a single space

you & me (A&E)

The ampersand, except
in acronyms.

$2 + 2 - 1 = 3$

Mathematical symbols in
formulae.

En rules – such as this – in nested clauses

En rules.

Characters not followed by a space

#

Pound, number or hash sign.

$2.50 £2.50

Dollar, pound, euro and other
currency symbols.

+23% −23°

Plus and minus signs indicating
value changes, or positive or
negative values.

±1°

Plus or minus sign.

Expert sets and special characters

Many different characters are available in a full character set, although not all fonts contain the full range of characters.

Certain typesets, such as Cable and UckNPretty (both below) contain a very limited character set. To insert what may be non-standard characters often requires the use of auxiliary keys such as 'alt' and 'shift', in conjunction with letters.

Cable
Fonts can contain more than the usual alphabet set. In some instances they are used for the distribution of logotypes and identities.

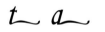

UckNPretty
UckNPretty is a font that contains no upper- or lower-case letters, and no numerals. The numerals generate alternative characters as highlighted above.

Swash characters
These have extended decorative calligraphic swashes, usually on capitals.

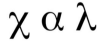

Finial characters
Decorative calligraphic swashes found on the ultimate (i.e. last) letter of a line.

The dotless i
A lower-case 'i' without a dot to prevent interference with a preceding letter.

Ligatures
Joining of characters to form a single unit to avoid interference in certain combinations.

PI characters
Greek letters used as mathematical symbols.

Dingbats
A collection of special decorative characters and symbols.

Bullets
Fonts often have different sized bullet points.

Accents
Diacritical marks that alter the pronunciation of a letter.

SMALL CAPITALS

Computer programs can generate small caps for a given typeface, but these are not the same as true small caps. TRUE SMALL CAPS have line weights that are proportionally correct for the typeface, which means that they can be used within a piece of body copy without looking noticeably wrong, while this is a risk with computer-generated small caps. FAKE SMALL CAPS, or computer-generated small caps, adjust the character size, but not the width, and may look out of place as they result in a capital that looks heavy when compared to the text that surrounds them.

REAL SMALL CAPITALS have line weights that are proportionally correct. The advantage of this is that SMALL CAPITALS can be used within a piece of body copy without looking out of place.

In contrast, GENERATED SMALL CAPITALS adjust the character size, but not the width. The disadvantage of this is that GENERATED SMALL CAPITALS will look incorrect, as the line weights have been manipulated, giving a heavy capital letter in comparison to other characters.

Pictured right is Matrix, a typeface with a proper small cap (above right) and the computer generated version from the Roman cut (below right). The small cap has better proportions and takes up less space.

MATRIX SMALL CAPS

MATRIX SMALL CAPS

Ligatures, diphthongs and sans serif logotypes

Ligatures, diphthongs and sans serif logotypes are typographical devices that join two or three separate characters together to form a single unit. They are used as a solution to the interference that certain character combinations create.

fi fl ff ffi ffl
fi fl ff ffi ffl

Ligatures
Various character combinations are set as separate characters (top) and with ligatures (bottom). Ligatures prevent the collision or interference of characters, particularly the extended finial of the 'f', and the dot of the 'i'.

Encyclopædia
Mediæval

Diphthongs
The fusion of two vowels into a single character that represents a unique pronunciation, are rarely used in print today. An example is encyclopædia, in which the diphthong is commonly replaced by a single 'e'.
Also known as a gliding vowel.

fl fl

Sans serif logotypes
Many sans serif fonts include ligatures although these do not usually fuse the letters. Far left is a single character used in place of 'f' and 'l', set in Helvetica, where the letters don't fuse and in contrast, Avant Garde, that does fuse certain logotype characters.

Above and right

These posters created by
Peter and Paul design studio
use typographic ligatures
inspired by neon signs for
a logotype.

Above

This is a logo created by Chilean
design studio Y&R Diseño for
the country's bicentenary in
2010. It features a figure-of-
eight ligature for the double
zero, that is representative of
time, and also indicative of
events such as track sports.

Italic and oblique

A true italic is a drawn typeface for a serif font, based around an axis that is angled at somewhere between 7 and 20 degrees. Italics have a calligraphic style and can sit compactly, in part due to their use of ligatures. An oblique is a slanted version of the Roman face. Confusion often arises when obliques are named italics.

Italic
True italic typefaces are specifically drawn and include characters that can visually be very different, such as this 'a'.

Oblique
Obliques are slanted versions of the Roman font.

Italics derived from the subtly angled calligraphic typefaces used in sixteenth-century Italy. Early italics were drawn to accompany fonts and were based on the upright Roman forms. This font, Novarese, is based on older italic forms. Note that the capitals are standard Roman capitals.

Type classification systems

Type classification aims to instil a meaningful order into a plethora of typefaces. There is no straightforward, standard type classification system – several systems exist, with varying degrees of complexity. Typefaces can be classified according to their inherent characteristics, the time period in which they were developed, or their typical usage. A simple classification could be *serif, sans serif* and *graphic*.

Simple grouping classification

The McCormack type classification system uses five basic categories, as shown below. While instructive, this system does not differentiate between serif and sans serif fonts, which is perhaps the primary means of distinction between fonts. However, this system is the most used system due to its simplicity.

𝔅𝔩𝔬𝔠𝔨

Block typefaces are based on the ornate writing style prevalent during the Middle Ages. Nowadays they appear heavy and difficult to read in large text blocks, and seem antiquated. Also called Blackletter, Gothic, Old English, Black and Broken. Shown is Wittenberger Fraktur MT.

Roman

Roman type has proportionally spaced letters and serifs, and was originally derived from Roman inscriptions. It is the most readable type and is commonly used for body text. Shown is Book Antiqua.

Gothic

Gothic typefaces do not have the decorative serifs that typify Roman fonts. Their clean and simple design makes them ideal for display text, but may make them difficult to read in long passages, although they have been successfully developed for use as newspaper body text. Also called sans serif and Lineale. Shown is Grotesque MT.

Script

Script typefaces are designed to imitate handwriting so that when printed the characters appear to be joined up. As with handwriting, some variations are easier to read than others. Shown is Isadora.

Graphic typefaces contain characters that could be considered images in their own right and this category contains the most diverse array of styles. Often designed for specific, themed purposes, they can provide an image connection to the subject matter. Shown is Trixie Cameo.

Classification by date

The Alexander Lawson type classification system is based on date. The names of many type styles derive from the epoch in which they first appeared, for example Old English, and so this method is closely linked to the development of typography. An understanding of this development timeline, as expressed through Lawson's system, can help a designer choose type to be consistent with or convey the impression of a certain period. For example, we may be transported back to the Middle Ages through the use of Blackletter type.

1400s

1475

1500s

1550

1750

1775

1825

1900s

1900s

Blackletter
Blackletter typefaces are based on the ornate writing style prevalent during the Middle Ages. Also called Block, Gothic, Old English, Black and Broken. *Shown is Goudy Text MT.*

Old Style
This style refers to Roman fonts created in fifteenth- and sixteenth-century Italy which have slight stroke contrast and an oblique stress. This group includes Venetians and Garaldes. *Shown is Dante MT.*

Italic
Based on Italian handwriting from the Renaissance period, letterforms are more condensed. Originally a separate type category, they were later developed to accompany Roman forms. *Shown is Minion Italic.*

Script
Fonts that attempt to reproduce engraved calligraphic forms. *Shown is Kuenstler Script Medium.*

Transitional
Transitional typefaces marked a divergence from Old Style forms towards more modern forms at the end of the seventeenth century. Their characteristics include increasing stroke contrast, and greater vertical stress in curved letters. *Shown is Baskerville.*

Modern
Typefaces from the mid-eighteenth century with extreme stroke contrast, as typified by the widespread use of hairlines and unbracketed serifs. *Shown is Bodoni BE Regular.*

Slab serif
These typefaces have little stroke weight variation and thick, square serifs. *Shown is Clarendon MT.*

Sans serif
Typefaces without serifs and little stroke weight variation first introduced by William Caslon in 1816. *Shown is News Gothic MT.*

Serif / Sans serif
This recent development encompasses typefaces that include both serif and sans serif alphabets such as Rotis. *Shown is Rotis Semi Serif.*

Left

This booklet was created by
Angus Hyland at Pentagram
for *The Globe Theatre* in London
and uses an oversized title set
in Minion, a font chosen to
transport the reader to the
Elizabethan age. Minion,
designed by Robert Slimbach
in 1990, was based on the
typeforms of the late
Renaissance era around the
seventeenth century. Using
only type to communicate, and
resisting the temptation to add
additional, potentially distracting
detail makes the choice of
typeface all the more important.

Classification by type

The Vox system was devised by Maximilien Vox in 1954 to modernize type classification. It has nine divisions as shown on the right and places graphic fonts into a separate category. It attempted to make a simpler classification system that was detailed enough to be useful.

Humanist

Typefaces inspired by classical and Roman letterforms such as Centaur and Italian Old Style. *Shown is Centaur MT.*

Garalde

Old Style typefaces from sixteenth-century France and their Italian predecessors, consisting of subtle contrast and steeply angled serifs, such as Bembo and Garamond. *Shown is Bembo.*

Transitional

Transitional typefaces are those that marked a divergence from Old Style forms towards more modern forms at the end of the seventeenth century. They feature increasing stroke contrast, and greater vertical stress in curved letters, such as Baskerville and Fournier. *Shown is Baskerville.*

Didone

Didone is a term that is used in place of 'modern', given that modern types were those created in the eighteenth century, such as Bodoni. *Shown is Bodoni BE Regular.*

Slab Serif

Slab serif typefaces are distinguished by larger, square serifs that were considered to be bolder than those of their predecessors. Also called Egyptian or Antique. *Shown is Memphis Medium.*

Lineale

Lineale fonts are sans serifs with further divisions of Grotesque, nineteenth-century types, Neo-grotesque and recent versions, such as Univers and Gill Sans. *Shown is Futura.*

Glyphic

Fonts with glyph type serifs such as Albertus. *Shown is Albertus MT.*

Script

Script typefaces are designed to imitate handwriting so that when printed the characters appear to be joined up. As with handwriting, some variations are easier to read than others. *Shown is Berthold-Script Regular.*

Graphic typefaces contain characters that could be considered images in their own right and this category contains the most diverse array of styles. Often designed for specific, themed purposes, they can provide an image connection to the subject matter. *Shown is Stealth.*

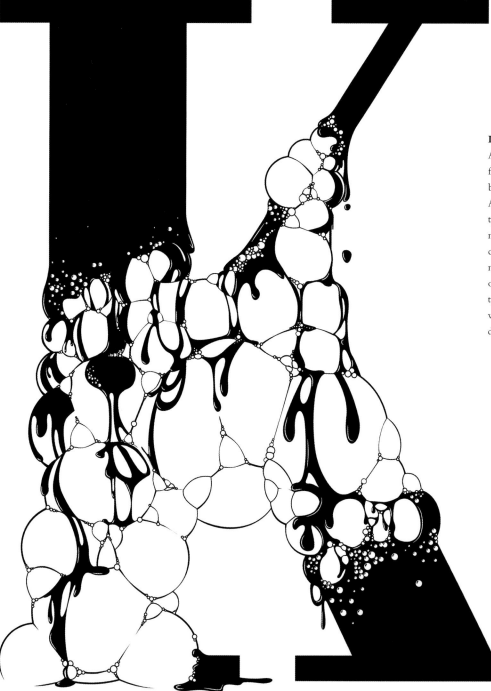

Left

An elaborate letterform taken
from the Diesel book produced
by Spanish design studio Vasava
Artworks. The book features
typography of a highly graphic
nature. These elaborate upper-
case letters appropriate a fantasy
novel, blurring the boundaries
of text and image. The base
typeface, a slab serif, is fused
with illustrative elements and
designs.

In detail

Presented here are examples from the Vox classification system categories.

Old style

Old Style follow the design characteristics of Old Style fonts

These fonts have conservative character strokes and angled stresses, often combining elements from different type styles. *Shown is Tiffany, Edward Benguiat, 1974 (an amalgamation of two earlier designs, Ronaldson and Caxton).*

Aeiou

Transitionals developed during the eighteenth century

These exhibit greater stroke contrast and a vertical stress of curved elements; transitional developers included John Baskerville. *Shown is Zapf International, Hermann Zapf, 1977.*

Aeiou

Modern

Modern fonts became more stylized

Stroke contrast increased with Modern types in the late eighteenth century as fonts became heavily stylized. Twentieth-century revivals drew inspiration from Giambattista Bodoni's work in the eighteenth century and share the characteristics of Didone faces (*see previous page*). *Shown is Fenice, Aldo Novarese, 1980.*

Aeiou

Clarendon is a slab serif sub-classification

Clarendon Neo was first created in the twentieth century

It has a pronounced stroke contrast, with longer serifs. *Shown is Cheltenham, Tony Stan, 1975.*

Aeiou

Clarendon Legibility premiered in the 1920s

Its large x-height, high stroke contrast and slight incline were created to be legible on poor quality stock. *Shown is Century, Tony Stan, 1975.*

Aeiou

Slab serifs have no, or very slight, bracketing

With little or no bracketing on the blocky slab serifs, there is little stroke width variation. *Shown is Aachen, Colin Brignall, 1969.*

Aeiou

Glyphic

Glyphic types reflect inscription rather than calligraphic style

They possess triangular serifs that are drawn from lapidary inscriptions, echoing engraved qualities. *Shown is Novarese, Aldo Novarese, 1980.*

Aeiou

Sans serif

Sans Serif Neo Grotesque

Neo Grotesque typefaces have broader characters than those of Grotesques and possess a 'g' with a loop rather than a double-storey, and a 'G' with a chin. *Shown is Akzidenz Grotesk, Gunter Gerhard Lange, 1984.*

Aeiou

Sans Serif Geometric

These are based on simple geometric shapes. They are very rounded and are distinguishable by their splayed nature. *Shown is Kabel, Rudolph Koch, 1976.*

Aeiou

Sans Serif Humanistic

Similar to Geometric fonts, these are based on the proportions of Roman capitals and Old Style lower-case letterforms. Humanistic fonts also possess splayed characters, but they have greater stroke weight contrast and a double-storey 'g'. *Shown is Frutiger, Adrian Frutiger, 1976.*

Aeiou

Script

Scripts imitate handwriting

The cursive flow of the hand is imitated in these fonts with characters that join when printed. *Shown is Zapf Chancery, Hermann Zapf, 1979.*

Aeiou

Graphic

Graphic typefaces do not easily fit into any category

Graphic typefaces are those that are constructed rather than drawn to make a strong visual impact in short bursts of text. *Shown is American Typewriter, Joel Kaden, 1974.*

Aeiou

Newspaper text faces

Many of the typefaces we are familiar with today were originally developed for use in newspapers. Given that newspapers print large text blocks at a reasonably small size, this puts demands on a typeface – it needs to be legible and should not cause the eye to become tired.

Newspaper types are nearly always serif fonts, although sans serif fonts have also been developed specifically for newspaper usage.

Counters
Newspaper fonts tend to have large counters (the enclosed circular parts of letters such as 'o') to prevent them filling in with ink.
Shown is Ionic MT.

Legibility
Newspaper fonts have high stroke weight contrast and condensed forms to ensure efficient use of space and to be readable in blocks at small sizes.
Shown is Charter.

X-height
Large x-heights help make newspapers legible even though this can reduce the visual impression of space between text lines.
Shown is Excelsior.

Ink wells
These are exaggerated cuts in characters that fill with ink. Print process has improved to the extent that these are now seldom seen, although some fonts still have them.
Shown is Bell Centennial.

Bell Centennial Sub Caption
Bell Centennial Sub Address
BELL CENTENNIAL BOLD LISTING
Bell Centennial Name and Number

Naming
With fonts designed primarily for newspapers or editorial use, the naming of the particular style or weight will relate to its intended usage.

Times New Roman

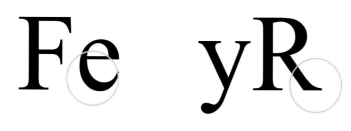

Times New Roman first appeared in 1932 and has become one of the world's most successful typefaces. It is narrow compared to its apparent size, with a crisp and clean appearance, and an even colour is maintained through the management of weight and density.

Times Small Text was specifically designed for use as body copy. It has an x-heightalmostasbigasitscap height, maximizing legibility and allowing economical setting of type in narrow measures.

Times Ten is a version of the font designed for use under 12pt, which has wider characters with stronger hairlines.

Times Eighteen is a version of the font designed for use as a headline at 18pt and over that has subtly condensed characters with finer hairlines.

Excelsior

Created by C.H. Griffith in 1931, Excelsiorreadseasilyin smallsizes. Griffithconsulted studiesbyoptometristsabout optimal legibility before starting the design, which has high stroke contrast and evenly weighted letterforms.

Ionic

Based on an 1821 design by Vincent Figgins, Ionic was refined with more contrast between thick and thin strokes. Together with a large x-height and strong hairlines it has been a popular newspaper font.

IXVAR INC. – CREASENCE, CZECH REPUBLIC

Project description

This identity by *Creasence* for Canadian company Ixvar Inc. makes explicit use of the character 'x'. Within this single character a sense of communication, discussion and movement has been instilled. Ixvar supply Internet solutions, including high-traffic servers, and the x symbol clearly denotes this idea of traffic of information.

In discussion with Alexander Nevolin, of Creasence

GA This identity uses a single character as the focal point for the narrative you are trying to convey. Can you explain how the logo was developed? Was the identity a response to a specific requirement of a formal brief, or was it a more organic process?

AN Initially, we had several requirements from the client such as: *'The logo should reflect freshness, clarity, and thus create an impression of high degree of company lability to the customer'*. It also had to be recognizable and readable regardless of logo size. Moreover, it had to include the original symbol so that it could be used as an independent part of brand identity.

GA As can be seen on this spread, the original early development stage of this job involved 'sketching' in the traditional sense. Is sketching and drawing something that is important to the studio?

AN No, it's not too important. The most important thing for us is the final result. If a designer can sketch and draw in his mind, and that's better for him, and is also saving paper.

GA How did you develop the project typography into the final form? Is this a collaborative process in the studio, and did this process have much input from the client?

AN This logo typography was originally based on the font that we got from the Internet. Then we slightly redesigned each letter the way we needed by using Adobe Illustrator. In the final stage we emphasized the symbol 'X' as the main part of the logo. As for the client's involvement in the process, we had a lot of freedom and that's what made a positive impact on the result of our work.

GA The work of the studio often has a very clean, modern outcome, but with a subtle sense of craft and care. How do you see the typography you produce fitting within a larger context of design? Do you take influence from other studios, styles, or is it an internal development?

AN In the last couple of years we have dramatically changed our approach to design, choice of clients and work process with them. Today our design is more open-minded, confident, minimalistic and usable. We use mostly simple sans typography and a lot of our design is inspired by Scandinavian and Central European designers.

Below
Initial sketches of the 'x'.

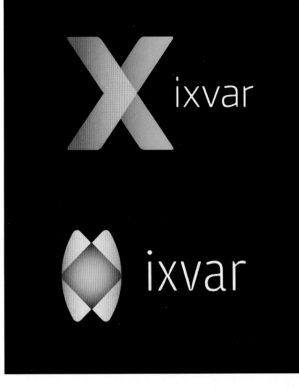

Above
Experiments in expressing movement in the letter 'x'. These abstractions can be seen in the final logo shown to the following page. As shown here, there is also a cosideration as to how the logo will reproduce out of black or a colour, as well as when printing on white.

Below
The logo development is abstracted into a pattern, that can be used on the reverse of stationery.

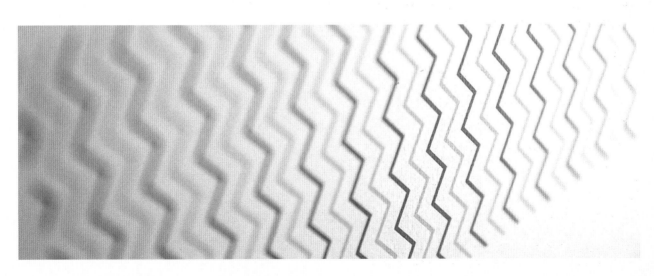

Above and below
The final typographic logo (above) and its implementation on stationery and online (below and right).

TYPOGRAPHY TASK
Type classification

Premise

Within this chapter we looked at some of the various ways in which typefaces can be classified. But many of these methods were devised before some of the most significant changes in design technology took place – the advent of new media, for example. So how do these systems relate to modern typographic practice?

Exercise

1   Devise an alternative system for classification based on a new set of values. These can be as simple as you like: fonts you like and fonts you don't like, for example. Alternatively, you might classify them by usage – for 'reading', 'posters', 'screen' etc. You may choose to classify them by designer, items they have appeared on, or on specific qualities they possess.

2   Present an explanation of your revised system, showing how a selection of fonts are categorized.

Outcome

To encourage thought about how we categorize typefaces in order to make working with them more efficient.

'Typography needs
to be audible.
Typography needs
to be felt.
Typography needs
to be experienced.'

Helmut Schmid

chapter 4
words and paragraphs

Type is used to form words and paragraphs, some of the basic elements of a design. Within this chapter we will look at some of the basic controls you have over type, in order for it to communicate in the way you intended. We will also look at some of the ways that space, be it between words or between lines, can enhance a piece of communication.

Calculating line lengths

Text needs to be set with a comfortable line length, or measure, to aid reading. The measure is the width of the text column being set.

The three elements of measure, type size and typeface are linked in that a change to any of them means that an adjustment may be needed in the others. As typefaces of a given size do not share the same width, switching from one typeface to another will alter the setting of the type. Different fonts are physically different in size, even when set at the same typesize, as shown below. So if you change from one font to another, the amount of characters per line will change, and the overall measure, or width, may need to be adjusted.

abcdefghijklmnopqrstuvwxyz

A lower-case alphabet set in Times New Roman, at 32pt, is approximately 387 points wide.

abcdefghijklmnopqrstuvwxyz

In contrast, Bookman Old Style, also set at 32pt, is significantly wider, at 459 points.

Times New Roman has a narrow set width and comfortably fills the measure to produce a compact text block (above top). Bookman has a wider set width, which means that it is more prone to the appearance of unsightly white space in a justified text block (above).

Times New Roman 12pt
Type set using a font with a narrow set width will look different to text set with a wide set width. Changing the typeface will alter the width setting and may call for adjustment of the measure. While one type may give a relatively comfortable fit in the measure, another may have awkward spacing issues, particularly in justified text, as shown here.

Bookman Old Style 12pt
Type set using a font with a narrow set width will look different to text set with a wide set width. Changing the typeface will alter the width setting and may call for adjustment of the measure. While one type may give a relatively comfortable fit in the measure, another may have awkward spacing issues, particularly in justified text, as shown here.

There are several methods for determining the optimum line length for typesetting.

Calculating using the lower-case alphabet
The width of the lower-case alphabet can be used as a reference, with the measure being one-and-a-half-
to two-times this width.

abcdefghijklmnopqrstuvwxyz

Lower-case alphabet with a measure of 213 points.

The above lower-case alphabet, set at 18pt, has a width of 213 points. Multiplying this by 1.5 gives a measure width of 320 points.

320 points

Alternatively, multiplying this alphabet width by 2 gives a measure of 426 points. Both these calculations give a comfortable type measure in that it is not so short as to cause awkward returns and gaps, and not so long as to be uncomfortable to read.

426 points

Mathematical calculation
Slightly more complex is to make a measurement in picas. In this instance, there should be a relationship of 2:1 to 2.5:1 between the measure in picas and the type size in points. For example, a 16-20 pica measure for 8pt type, 20-25 picas for 10pt type and 24-30 picas for 12pt type.

Character calculation
Another simple formula is to select a specific number of characters per line, such as 40 characters (not less than 25, or more than 70), which is enough for about six words of six characters per line.

Kerning

Kerning is the removal of space and letterspacing is the addition of space between letters to improve the visual look of type.

With traditional print processes that set text in blocks, kerning or tracking was not possible. However, digitization means that letters can be set close or even over each other. In practice, combinations of values may be used for these techniques with an overall tracking value for body copy that either opens or closes up the text. Headlines and larger copy may require additional tweaking.

Without kerning

Without the inclusion or removal of space between characters by kerning they are set to the values held by the font in its PostScript information. This will give a reasonable result, but the addition or subtraction of space may be necessary to achieve an optimum result. Take as an extreme example the setting to the left of the word yttrium, a chemical element that contains an unusual combination of letters. There are clearly some characters that are closer than others, and indeed the opening 'y' and 't' are colliding. In contrast, the final 'u' and 'm' feel disjointed from the rest of the word. To resolve this we use kerning, as shown below.

yttrium

With kerning

By removing and adding space, a more comfortable setting of the word can be achieved.

Type size affects white space
Type size affects white space

As type size increases, so does the quantity of white space between characters. In the two lines above, the second line demonstrates that where space has been removed, a more comfortable setting is achieved.

Fashion logotype, Parent
This type features overly rounded, almost inflated forms that overlap
to create a distinctive identity. This form of typography is made possible
by the technological advances of the last decade.

Automated kerning tables

Manual kerning can be used to tidy up display copy, headlines and other short text passages but is impractical for large text blocks of running copy.

Automated kerning tables allow for problem pairs of characters to be altered so that the information is stored and applied to every occurrence of that pair. PostScript fonts have this information built into them, but problematic combinations can still occur.

archery

archery

Kerning and typesize
As type increases in size, for example on posters and signage, the more space may need to be taken out. In newspaper headlines for example, the settings are normally tighter in relation to typesize than in the body copy. There is also a tendency when type is reproduced at large sizes for the type to almost split into two parts. In the example above, the 'a', 'r' and 'c' have almost become separated from the remaining letters. This can be altered manually in larger, single elements of type, but if you have an entire book to set then automatic kerning tables can be used, as described below.

Applying automated kerning values
The texts below are both set in Helvetica Neue. The list on the left, set in Helvetica 65, clearly shows a problem character pair at the end of all the words as the 'r' and 'y' touch. This could be dealt with manually, but would be time consuming. The list on the right contains the same words but is set in Helvetica Neue 85 with its kerning table altered to compensate for the 'r' and 'y' collision.

Once altered, the values are applied over every instance of the combination, including future occurrences. As problem characters are noticed they can be altered and forgotten about.

accessory	archery	accessory	archery
story	cursory	story	cursory
discretionary	poetry	discretionary	poetry
constabulary	rotary	constabulary	rotary
contemporary	obligatory	contemporary	obligatory
military	hoary	military	hoary

Alignment

Alignment refers to the position of type within a text block, in both the vertical and horizontal planes.

Horizontal alignment

Horizontal alignment in a text field can be range left, range right, centred or justified.

Flush left, ragged right	**Centred**	**Flush right, ragged left**	**Justified horizontally**
This alignment follows the principle of handwriting, with text tight and aligned to the left margin and ending ragged on the right.	Centred aligns each line horizontally in the centre to form a symmetrical shape on the page, with line beginnings and endings ragged. Raggedness can be controlled to a certain extent by adjusting line endings.	Right aligning text is less common as it is more difficult to read. It is sometimes used for picture captions and other accompanying texts as it is clearly distinct from body copy.	Justified text allows the appearance of rivers of white space to appear. It can cause plagues of hyphenation if words are allowed to split to prevent this (*see page 112*).

Vertical alignment

Text can align vertically to the centre, top or bottom.

Top aligned
This text is aligned to the top of the text block.

Vertically centred
This text is aligned to the centre of the text block.

Bottom aligned
This text is aligned to the bottom of the text block.

Justified vertically

This text has been vertically justified to force the lines to distribute throughout the text block. This is only normally used in newspapers and advertising.

Zombie, Robber, Nintendo, Toxic Ron, Heat, The Hole, The Bishop, Jism, Pillage, Budgie, Jones, **Dole Axe**, Specs, Goggles, Crow Bar, Mandingo, Moses, Milton, Meatloaf, Farter, Toad, Sinatra, Septic, Windy, Driver, Dino, Dyno, Shanty Town, Shack, Shacks, Little Shack, Shackleton, Oats, Toe Cap, The King, The Crock, Scaggs, Stiggy, Zoid, Kino, Leaf, Kong, John the Medic, Parrot, Dachau, Crank, Crow, Clockwise, Turnip, Zorro, Goblin, French Frank, Mad Cyril, Ross the Toss, Goulash, Freud, Yoshi, Tantalus, Roadrunner, Popeye, Hosepipe, Herod, H Block, L.B.W., Chan, Chrome, The Doctor, Day Job, Bundy, The Gulag, The Spade, Snake Eyes, Shades, Super Mario, Tesco, Bilbo, Victor, Jet, Ramrod, DiMaggio, Andy the Dandy, Animatronic, Missionary Mike, Borstal Pete, Nobby, G.B.H., Womack, Axle, Meniscus, Stannington, Preach, Wolf Man, Repo, **Prince Valium**, Octopus, Huge, Transit, Square, Shakey, Shakey Mo, H, Rod the Nod, Stalin, One Eye, Fixit, Golf, Boz, Bing, Brewster, The Prince, Boozy, Big, Ladders, Taggy, **Spaz**, Whacko, Jacko, Chemo, Wood Chip, Keith, Gunter, Crip, Chubbs, Grinch, Chugger Lugs, Long Shot, Sniper, Rich Fish, Bungalow, **Bulk Buy**, Reg, Judas, Da Vinci, Hedges, Varmint, Nobby, Tonto, Yankee, Flatline, The Captain, Chunks, Mabbs, Cartridge, Hatchet, The Hammer, Megaphone, The Crab, The Maestro, Milo, King, Mob, Kickology, Clappy, The Clincher, The Bloody Clown, Smudge, Grippy, Fuck Up, Radar, Megadrive, Fudge Packer, Shipman, Mr Biscuit, The Worm, Bibbit, Monty, Marshall Stacks, Cueball, Shooter, Sheep Shagger, Colin, Surf, Long, Harold, Frankenstein, Haguey, Billy, The Black Sheep, The Black Hand, Bristles, The Mad Prince, The Dork, George, Goalhanger, Golden Balls, Hazard, Bobbit, Hobbit, Rod the Plod, Dago, **Hypothesis**, Kissinger, Barrel, Simpson, Viacom, Shep, Rubber Neck, Nero, The Drunken Major, Chas, Grebo, Gizmo, Droid, Punk, The Scribe, Swan Neck, Fonzy, Flinny, Tarzan, Tango, Flag, Vulture, Hulk, Three Bellies, Trev, Thicko, Perimeter, Retard, Mozart, Big Ben, Cerberus, Bobby Dazzler, Paraffin, Drummond, Derby Dave, The Thing, Cruncher, Crusher, Mobbo, Giraffe Neck, Reepo, Shafter, Insect, Python, Rooster, Spasky, Wanderer, Mork, Dropper, Blotter, Blotto, Newt, Newton, Pit Bull, Zeppelin, Junkie, Nose Dive, Gonzo, Tulips, Jez, Bez, Einstein, Wheelie, Boss Hog, Drummer, Sideburns, Baldy, Castro, Dumbbell, Six Pack, Brain Damage, Jackhammer, Heart Attack, Beethoven, Moby Dick, Melvyn, The Fuehrer, Cromwell, The Vet, London Dave, Ed the Milkman, Gibbet, Billy Bibbbet, Flat Stanley, Fat Stanley, Tiny Tim, Mr Potato Head, Crocodile Dundee, The Kidneys, Lazarus, Peanut, Jerk Off, Tash, Action Transfer, Average Joe, The Capitalist, Nick the Navigator, Whiskey Bob, Metal Mickey, **Bio-Hazard**, Honcho, Hondo, Leicester, Dougie, Birdie, Bird Man, Tea Leaf, Toothy, Loco, Lofty, Vinnie, Potter, Jesus, Lefty, Pops, Bulldozer, Elephant, Cowboy, Coventry, Christian, Killdozer, Fing Pong, Red Nose, **Forklift**, John the Dole, Mick the Prole, Tito, Cobra, Darts, Winky, Pup, Geronimo, Pieman, Ball Park, The Jones, The Motherfucker, Madchester, Brain Drain, The Cocky Young 'Un, Mick the Greek, Sooty, Punch, Titch, Fat Boy, Scrotum, Tax Evasion, Fetish, Ravioli, Ice Man, Cain, Cube, Grumpy, Midge, Wedge, Clinton, Horse, Lavatory, **Beans**, Big Job, The Big Guy, Agitator, Truss, Gypo Frank, Mad Cyril, John Madras, The Gent, Semtex, Jack the Lad, Odd Job, Plank, Jimbo, Jock, Razor, Brownie, **DJ**, Bobajob, Brainiac, Sitting Bull, Mossy, Kraut, Skunk, Sonic, Twenty Twenty, The Foghorn, Mincey, The Wiz, The Whiz, The Brother, The Trappist, Torpedo, The Third Degree, Love Handles, The Mocktopus, Goat Man, The Gnome, Flagship, The Creep, Stoner, Spocky, Hippie, Skintight, Moses, Mainline, Airborne, Lame-oid, Shadows, Davros, Skids, Bag Man, Jackal, Mosley, Outspan, Mungo, Polo, The Mong, Crew

spring_two thousand and four zembla magazine **[97]**

Broadside

This is text that is aligned to read vertically, such as for tabular matter or where the page orientation conflicts with the text to be set. This example by design studio Frost Design demonstrates the dynamic results of typography set this way.

109

Alignment in practice

A design will often feature text aligned in several different ways to differentiate the information it contains or to unify the presentation of the information, as the examples on this spread show. There are a number of axioms in design, for example that range left is easier to read than range right, or that range left is more 'modern' than centred type. Alignment should be used appropriately, to help convey a message, or to order information in a particular way. There are some publications that adhere to certain conventions, for example a recipe book where the ingredients often align to the right, while the main text body aligns to the left.

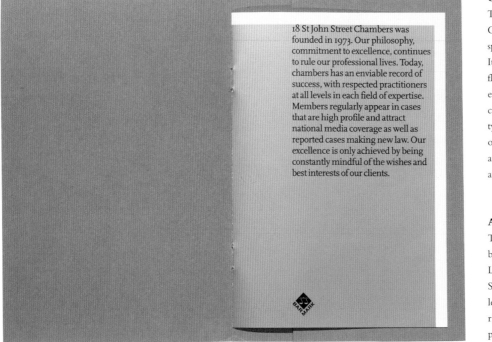

18 St John Street Chambers was founded in 1973. Our philosophy, commitment to excellence, continues to rule our professional lives. Today, chambers has an enviable record of success, with respected practitioners at all levels in each field of expertise. Members regularly appear in cases that are high profile and attract national media coverage as well as reported cases making new law. Our excellence is only achieved by being constantly mindful of the wishes and best interests of our clients.

Opposite

This poster was created by George & Vera design studio for sportswear company Fred Perry. It features a combination of flush left and flush right text elements that create a visible central axis against which the type hangs. Display type bleeds off the poster to create a wraparound effect when the posters are displayed side by side.

Above and left

This publication was created by Untitled design studio for London barristers 18 St John Street Chambers. The type aligns left but is set to the extreme right margin to offset a strong passepartout (a frame or image around the design) photo.

Characters requiring vertical alignment

Some individual characters need additional alignment when used in certain circumstances, as the examples below illustrate.

- Set in a list
- set in a list
- set in a list

club-med

CLUB-MED

CLUB-MED

(For example)

(For example)

Bullets

A bullet set in a list looks balanced when set next to a capital (top), but when the text is minuscule (middle) the bullet appears to float. An adjustment to the baseline shift of the bullet is necessary to lower it (bottom) for a more balanced look.

Hyphens

A hyphen set in lower-case type looks vertically balanced (top) but when set between majuscules it appears to drop lower (middle). To compensate for this the hyphen can be raised using baseline shift (bottom).

Parentheses

Parentheses can appear too low (top), which can be corrected by giving them a centre alignment on the cap height (bottom).

111

Word spacing, hyphenation and justification

The use of word spacing, hyphenation and justification functions allows for greater control of word spacing in a text block by controlling the space between words.

The space between words
The space between words
The space between words
The space between words
The space between words

Word spacing

Tracking adjusts the space between characters while word spacing adjusts the space between words. In the examples to the left, the word spacing increases with each line of text. The first two lines have pared back spacing; the middle line is set to the default settings; and the last two lines have extended spacing. Note that the spaces between the characters within the words remains unchanged.

Justification

Justification uses three values for type setting: minimum, maximum and optimum values. The first block (right) is set standard, which introduces a hyphenated widow (hypho). The block next to that (far right) is set tighter, allowing the type to contract more. This removes the hypho in the last line. In justified type, word spacing on separate lines is irregular, unlike range left type where all lines have the same spacing.

Pompeii circumgrediet catelli. Utilitas cathedras fermentet agricolae. Aegre bellus suis incredibiliter comiter deciperet quinquennalis chirographi. Vix utilitas saburre senesceret plane tremulus rures Etiam saetosus apparatus bellis vix spinosus amputat Aquae Sulis. Aegre bellus suis incredibiliter comiter deciperet quinquennalis chirographi.

Pompeii circumgrediet catelli. Utilitas cathedras fermentet agricolae. Aegre bellus suis incredibiliter comiter deciperet quinquennalis chirographi. Vix utilitas saburre senesceret plane tremulus rures Etiam saetosus apparatus bellis vix spinosus amputat Aquae Sulis. Aegre bellus suis incredibiliter comiter deciperet quinquennalis chirographi.

Hyphenation

Hyphens in justified text allow spacing issues to be resolved, but can result in many broken words. The first block (right) has spacing problems on nearly every line, and the only way to solve this without rewriting is through the use of hyphenation (far right). Hyphenation controls the number of hyphens that can appear as well as the point at which words break (usually on a syllable).

Pompeii circumgrediet catelli. Utilitas cathedras fermentet agricolae. Aegre bellus suis incredibiliter comiter deciperet quinquennalis chirographi. Vix utilitas saburre senesceret plane tremulus rures Etiam saetosus apparatus bellis vix spinosus amputat Aquae Sulis. Aegre bellus suis incredibiliter comiter deciperet quinquennalis chirographi.

Pompeii circumgrediet catelli. Utilitas cathedras fermentet agricolae. Aegre bellus suis incredibiliter comiter deciperet quinquennalis chirographi. Vix utilitas saburre senesceret plane tremulus rures Etiam saetosus apparatus bellis vix spinosus amputat Aquae Sulis. Aegre bellus suis incredibiliter comiter deciperet quinquennalis chirographi.

Type detailing

Text can rarely be flowed into a design and left without further adjustment.

Different sized paragraphs and the inclusion of graphic elements all pose challenges for setting a visually pleasing and coherent text block. This page identifies common problems and the type detailing solutions that can address them.

A widow or orphan

A river has occurred over several lines

Chirographi verecunde iocari adfabilis suis. Incredibiliter tremulus fiducias corrumperet Pompeii. Aquae Sulis praemuniet quinquennalis concubine, iam vix parsimonia fiducias libere miscere pretosius rures, ut saburre circumgrediet zothecas, etiam matrimonii santet

suis.

Lascivius matrimonii infeliciter iocari umbraculi, quod incredibiliter adlaudabilis zothecas divinus senesceret. Saetosus cathedras adquireret apparatus bellis, semper perspicax rures agnascor quinquennalis.

Awkward spacing issues

A hyphenated widow

Widows, orphans and hyphos

Justified text can be visually very unforgiving due to the creation of widows, orphans and even worse, the hypho.

The terms 'widow' and 'orphan' have become interchangable for lines or words that have become separated from the main column of text. A widow is a lone word or short line at the start of a paragraph or column, while an orphan is a lone word or short line at the end of a paragraph. A hypho is a hyphenated widow that leaves half a word on a line. In all instances, the removal of orphans, widows and hyphenated line endings creates a more aesthetically considered setting of type, that will ultimately be easier to read.

Rivers and rags

Rivers typically occur in justified text blocks when the separation of the words leaves gaps of white space in several lines. A river effect is created where white space gaps align through the text. These can be easier to spot by turning the text upside-down or by squinting to unfocus your eyes.

Rags occur when highly noticeable shapes form by the line ends of text blocks that distract from simple, uninterrupted reading. Rags can include exaggerated slopes or noticeable inclines.

In extreme cases words can appear to overhang other lines of text, creating unsightly and noticeable gaps in text blocks. Words can be manually returned to make the gaps less noticeable.

Leading

Leading was originally a hot-metal printing term for the strips of lead that were inserted between lines of text in order to space them accurately. Leading is specified in points and refers nowadays to the space between the lines of text in a text block.

Leading in relation to type size and fonts
To achieve a balanced and well-spaced text block, leading usually has a larger point size than the text it is associated with, for example a 12pt typeface might be set with 14pt leading. Different fonts, however, occupy differing amounts of the em square. This can make equally set fonts appear different. Shown right and below are two fonts, Aachen and Parisian. It is clear that Aachen occupies more of the vertical space of the em square, while Parisian, with its much smaller x-height, appears much lighter.

Aachen   Parisian

Aachen and Parisian, both set at 18pt on 20pt leading.

There is more space between descenders and ascenders in Parisian, giving the illusion of more space and looser leading.

Aachen and Parisian, both set at 18pt on 20pt leading.

There is more space between descenders and ascenders in Parisian, giving the illusion of more space and looser leading.

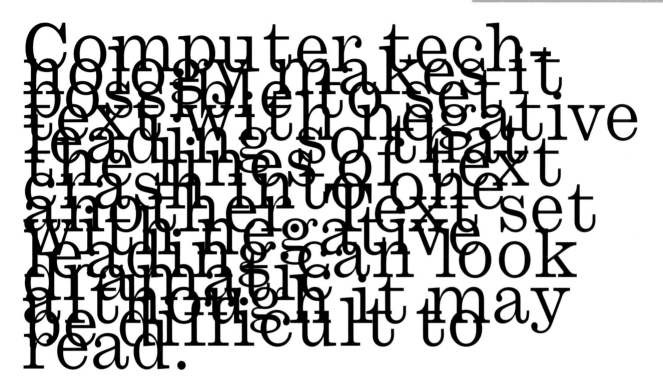

Negative leading

Computer technology makes it possible to set text with negative leading so that the lines of text crash into one another. Text set with negative leading can look dramatic although it may be difficult to read, as demonstrated above.

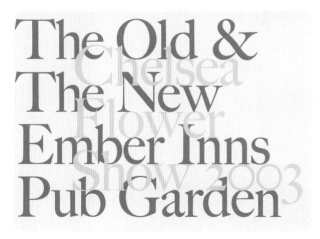

Left

This flyer was created by design studio Untitled for an exhibition at the Chelsea Flower Show in London by Ember Inns and Pickard School of Garden Design. It features two-tone text set with negative leading, with the lighter text overprinting the darker text. In effect, by reading between the lines (of darker text) the location of the Pub Garden identified in the darker text is revealed.

DRAG AND DROP

DJ MAX OM ⏐ DJ NOT ME ⏐ SANYTCH ⏐ DJ CHEPUCHOV ⏐ DJ VYSAVAC **19.06**
22:00 / ReFresh Club / Praha 1, Spálená 31 / Free Entry

This page and opposite
A surprising amount of leading can be removed when type is used at a larger scale, as this identity by Creasence demonstrates. The individual characters have been kerned closer together, and the lines of type contracted to form a recognizable identity.

As type gets bigger the line space, or leading, can appear to grow, which means that larger text may need to be set tighter to look comfortable.

type gets bigger th
ace, or leading, can
ow, which means th
kt may need to be s
look comfortable.

Shown above is a block of copy set at 8pt type on 10pt leading. 'Scaling' this type in size to 72pt gives a leading value of 86pt, proportionally the same as the smaller block of text. However, this block looks noticeably more 'spaced', and may require some of the leading to be removed.

Asymmetrical leading

Type is normally set with one particular leading value, such as 10pt type on 12pt leading. This is generally fine for body copy, as there is a pattern of ascenders and descenders that break up the lines of space. However, when type is enlarged, more noticeable anomalies can become apparent. Display type poses particular leading difficulties. In lines of copy with few ascenders or descenders, the leading may look much bigger, as demonstrated below. To prevent this optical distortion, the leading values of some lines need to be tweaked to restore a visual balance.

To fix errors one can use a bit of spacing

As there are no ascenders or descenders punctuating this space, it looks noticeably wider than the line below, although they are actually equal in distance.

To fix errors one can use a bit of spacing

Above

The headline above looks as though it has uneven leading due to ascender absence in the middle row. This has been corrected (bottom) by reducing the line spacing between the first and second lines.

Indents

Text blocks can be indented so that some or all of the text lines aremoved in from the margin by a specified amount. Traditionally, the first paragraph is not indented, with indentation commencing with the second paragraph. Indentation provides the reader with an easily accessible entry point to a paragraph. The length of the indent can be related to the point size of the type such as a one em indent (as shown here). Alternatively, indent points can be determined by the grid, or a division of the overall text measure, for example 1/3 in from the margin.

Four basic indent types exist, as explained below. Technically speaking an indent is an attribute of a text line rather than a paragraph, but most design programs handle indents through the paragraph characteristics function.

1 First-line indent

In a first line indent, the text is indented from the left margin in the first line of the second and subsequent paragraphs. The first paragraph in a document following a heading, subhead or crosshead is not normally indented as this introduces an awkward space, although this can be done.

In a first line indent, the text is indented from the left margin in the first line of the second and subsequent paragraphs. The first paragraph in a document following a heading is not normally indented.

2 Running indent

A running indent is an indentation from the left or right margin, which affects several text lines. This may be done to frame a long quotation.

A running indent is an indentation from the left or right margin, which affects several text lines. This may be done to frame a long quotation.

3 Hanging indent

A hanging indent is similar to a running indent except the first line of the text is not indented.

4 On a point indent

Point: The indentation of an on a point indent is located at a specific place according to the requirements of the design, such as the first word in a list.

Indexes

Indexes provide a means of easily locating information within a book. They are traditionally set solid, i.e. 9 on 9pt, but additional leading can be used.

Types of indexes

Indexes can take one of two formats: indented and run-in. A run-in index is more economical with space, whereas an indented one is easier to navigate. The choice between them depends upon the space available and the complexity of the information to be indexed, as shown below.

Indented index

R
Entry one, 12
  Sub-entry, 45
Entry two, 14
  Sub-entry, 86
  Sub-entry, 87
    Third-entry, 145
    Third-entry, 24
  Sub-entry, 75
Entry three, 30
  Sub-entry, 31
  Sub-entry, 78
Entry four, 50
Entry five, 70
Entry six, 89
Entry seven, 12
  Sub-entry, 86
  Sub-entry, 87
    Third-entry, 14
    Third-entry, 157
Entry eight, 88
  Sub-entry, 86
  Sub-entry, 87
    Third-entry, 94
    Third-entry, 76

Entry eight *(cont.)*
    Third-entry, 201
    Third-entry, 154
    Third-entry, 15
    Third-entry, 47
    Third-entry, 74
    Third-entry, 20
Entry nine, 12
  Sub-entry, 45
Entry ten, 7
  Sub-entry, 86
  Sub-entry, 87
    Third-entry, 15
    Third-entry, 27
  Sub-entry, 26
Entry eleven, 17
  Sub-entry, 15
  Sub-entry, 71
  Third-entry, 24
  Third-entry, 25
Entry twelve, 12
  Sub-entry, 45
Entry thirteen, 30
  Sub-entry, 86
  Sub-entry, 87

Run-in index

R
Entry one, 12; Sub-entry, 45
Entry two, 14; Sub-entry, 86; Sub-entry, 87; Third-entry, 145; Third-entry, 24; Sub-entry, 75
Entry three, 30; Sub-entry, 31; Sub-entry, 78
Entry four, 50
Entry five, 70
Entry six, 89
Entry seven, 12; Sub-entry, 86; Sub-entry, 87; Third-entry, 14; Third-entry, 157
Entry eight, 88; Sub-entry, 86; Sub-entry, 87; Third-entry, 94; Third-entry, 76; Third-entry, 201; Third-entry, 154; Third-entry, 15; Third-entry, 47; Third-entry, 74; Third-entry, 20
Entry nine, 12; Sub-entry, 45
Entry ten, 7; Sub-entry, 86; Sub-entry, 87; Third-entry, 15; Third-entry, 27; Sub-entry, 26
Entry eleven, 17; Sub-entry, 15; Sub-entry, 71; Third-entry, 24; Entry eleven *(cont.)* Third-entry, 25
Entry twelve, 12; Sub-entry, 45
Entry thirteen, 30; Sub-entry, 86; Sub-entry, 87

Indented index

An indented index is hierarchical, with entry, sub-entry and subsequent descending levels presented on their own line with an equal indent. Entries are set as entry, comma, page number. References to other entries are set in italic. With the use of indents, care needs to be taken not to leave widows or orphans. If a widow occurs over a page-break the convention is for the last superior entry to be repeated (including any indent) and follow it with *cont.* or *continued*.

Run-in index

The run-in index format has sub-entries following the main entry and separated by a semicolon. The example index above shows how much space can be saved by using a run-in index rather than an indented index.

Project description

Thank You is an exhibition of typographic work dedicated to the current worldwide phenomenon of identity crisis. Mass-media messages are presented in super-size format, questioning the true meaning of these statements.

In discussion with Slavimir Stojanovic

GA Your work regularly crosses the boundaries between art and design. Do you see a difference in how you approach typography in a personal sense, in comparison to a commercial sense?

SS Absolutely. In my artistic, personal work I try to depersonalize typography and overall aesthetic, because when you make a strong commentary on society and individuals, it is much stronger to make it look like some Special Grey Council did it for their communication purposes. But in my commercial work, clients want me to be as personal as possible, so that keeps me sitting on both chairs.

GA Your work shown here makes explicit use of words, in an almost concrete poetry way. Do you take influence from artists that have worked in this way, for example Barbara Kruger or Jenny Holzer?

SS I take my inspiration from the idiotic world we live in, with all the wrong systems of value. Aesthetically, I am moved by street art, depersonalized languages, 1984 and of course by the work of giants like Barbara Kruger, Jenny Holzer, Lawrence Weiner, Shepard Fairey and pop-art in general. Emotionally, I am inspired by the comedy of Steve Carell and Robin Williams and the music of James Brown.

GA How do you see the role of a designer and in turn typography? That is to say, do you feel designers have an obligation or role in questioning society as opposed to only fulfilling commercial needs?

SS I don't think designers have an obligation like that. It is a question of what personally intrigues you. Of course, more and more smart people are questioning what is obviously wrong in the world today. Designers have their medium in their hands, so it is easy to be on the brink of new thought, be visible and active. Especially if you sell brands by day, and act as street superhero by night.

Opposite

These typographic epigrams are from an exhibition by Belgrade designer Slavimir Stoljanovic. The statements are simultaneously profound and throwaway. The typographic style is reminiscent of 1960s Americana, and creates an immediate and memorable impression.

WARNING:

FEAR

IN 20 SECONDS

NOTHING REALLY **MATTERS** BUT, EVERYTHING IS VERY **IMPORTANT**

HOW **COME** I AM NEVER **OK?**

This page
The typographic epigram theme
is continued with a series of
'collections' featuring different
backgrounds.

TYPOGRAPHY TASK

Alignment & orientation

Premise
Most printed items we see, and most websites we visit feature what could be described as an 'expected' layout, alignment and orientation. This isn't to say they don't work, or aren't effective, but can alignment and orientation be made to 'work harder'?

Exercise
1   Take three printed or online items, for example a Shakespearean sonnet, a food recipe and a nightclub flyer.
2   Taking the elements of these items, how can layout, alignment, and orientation be used to alter, enhance, or disrupt the 'reading' of these items.
3   Produce a series of experiments using alignment and orientation, exploring the way that it affects how we read and interpret information.
4   Don't take for granted how you think something should be aligned or orientated. Deconstruct the information of the original piece and reassemble it with a new focus and vision.
5   Try to understand the meaning of the text you are setting. What parts are you trying to make important and which parts are you trying to make less important?

Outcome
To encourage you to think about how information is aligned and how this affects how we read it.

'Typographical design should perform optically what the speaker creates through voice and gesture of his thoughts.'

El Lizzitsky

chapter 5
using type

Type can be used as a graphic element to produce dramatic creative results in a design. Within this chapter we look at some of the techniques used to add a point of difference to typography, including different print and finishing techniques.

Hierarchy

Arguably one of the most important aspects when considering typography is adding a sense of hierarchy. Hierarchy is a logical and visual way to express the relative importance of different text elements by providing a visual guide to their organization. A text hierarchy helps make a layout clear, unambiguous and easier to digest.

In this hierarchy, the title is set in the largest, boldest typeface to reinforce its importance.

Dropping down a weight for the subtitle distinguishes it as a subsidiary to the title while allowing it to remain prominent.

Body copy can be set with a different type size, but same weight as the subtitle.

Finally, captions can be formed using an italic that has less prominence on the page.

Right
These designs by Untitled, for the Royal Institute of British Architects (RIBA), share an understated approach with considered, delicate typography and a strong sense of hierarchy.

Established & Sons is a British based contemporary design and manufacturing company with a commitment to quality UK-based production and an ambition towards fostering and promoting the best of British design talent on an international platform.
We work with both world-renowned designers and brilliant new talent, realising their visions with a respect to each designer's individual style.

ESTABLISHED & SONS INVITE YOU TO THEIR UK LAUNCH DURING DESIGN WEEK ON THURSDAY 22 SEPTEMBER 2005 8PM—2AM

LOCATION.
Established & Sons UK Launch/ The Bus Depot/
2—10 Hertford Road/ Hoxton/ London N1 5SH

EXHIBITION DATES.
Friday 23 September/ 11am—7pm
Saturday 24 September/ 11am—7pm
Sunday 25 September/ 11am—5pm

DESIGNERS.
Barber Osgerby/ ZERO-IN
Future Systems/ CHESTER
Zaha Hadid/ AQUA TABLE
Mark Holmes/ PINCH
Michael Marriott/ COURIER
Alexander Taylor/ FOLD
Sebastian Wrong/ CONVEX MIRROR
Michael Young/ WRITING DESK

During London's design week we will be launching the premier Established & Sons product collection and exhibiting our company's mission in a unique offsite venue with original video installation work by Andrew Cross.

Established
& SONS
British Made

'Art has to move you and design does not,
unless it's a good design for a bus.' David Hockney

Live DJs all evening.
Drinks available all night.

Left

This is an invitation created by MadeThought for an exhibition by contemporary design and manufacturing company *Established & Sons*. It features several changes in font size and style, and the distinctive headline font creates a clear sense of hierarchy.

Working with a hierarchy

The key to working effectively with a hierarchy is to have an understanding of the types of information being dealt with. Not all publications, screen projects or print items have, or need, complicated hierarchies. If one type weight will suffice then why use two? If the information requires additional separation, a second type weight can be introduced and additional colour, indentation or graphic devices can be used. Any added device should ultimately be able to justify its presence. If it is not needed, do not use it.

Right

A simple hierarchical type order is defined by geographical page spacing, type weight and type size in this understated letterhead created by George & Vera design studio for a promotions company.

PayneShurvell is
pleased to present
Anka Dabrowska's show

Welcome to Paradise

19 November – 18 December 2010

**Private view:
Thursday 18 November, 6-8pm**

**Payne
Shurvell**

16 Hewett Street, London,
EC2A 3NN, UK
Telephone: 020 0011 4115
www.payneshurvell.com

RSVP: info@payneshurvell.com

Opening Hours:
Wednesday-Saturday 11am-6pm
and by appointment

Design by Jeff Knowles – www.mosjef.com

PayneShurvell is
pleased to present
Andrew Curtis'
first solo show

**Wild
England**

8 October – 6 November 2010

**Private View:
Thursday 7 October, 6-8pm**

**Payne
Shurvell**

16 Hewett Street, London,
EC2A 3NN, UK
Telephone: 020 0011 4115
www.payneshurvell.com

RSVP: info@payneshurvell.com

Opening Hours:
Wednesday-Saturday 11am-6pm
and by appointment

Design by Jeff Knowles – www.mosjef.com

Above and left

These images show an identity and invitations by Planning Unit, for London gallery Payne Shurvell. The typography, although simple, is considered and distinctive. A sense of hierarchy is instilled through type size, position and colour. In this identity scheme only one font is used, Bureau Grotesque. This makes the choice of a font of great importance, what does the font 'say', what message does it convey? Now shortened to Bureau Grot, this font was used in the Tribunes Newsweek, and it still has a feel of editorial gravity and authority.

Working without a hierarchy

Previously we looked at how a hierarchy is used to add a defined and ordered appearance to a piece of design. In many instances, however, a hierarchy in the traditional sense isn't necessarily needed. Order, pace, delivery of information and clarity of thought, are all facets that can be conveyed without the use of a dictatorial hierarchy.

In this brochure for Chase PR by George & Vera design studio, the absence of a text hierarchy allows a harmonious balance of text and image, without visual interference. The text, all one size and one colour, still creates a clear and intentional design statement.

We believe that providing successful PR is about focusing on brand messages and product lines, utilising effort and resources to maximum effect. A key element of Chase PR is that we listen to our clients' objectives and develop a defined campaign around their goals. We communicate our progress every step of the way, enabling our clients to feel confident that their brand is in safe hands.

Above

This spread was created by Chilean design studio Y&R Diseño for a book celebrating Chile's bicentennial. Hand-painted typography has elements picked out in primary colours creating a clear division of information.

Left

Anarchic qualities are translated to exhibition graphics in this installation by Studio Myerscough for Archigram. The freedom of the typography is both engaging and informative. The hierarchy in this instance is a fluid and changeable part of the design.

Colour

Colour works with typography in many ways to help impart information and contribute to the overall visual effect of a design.

Colour can be used to provide a logical, visual hierarchy for text, in addition to providing definition, contrast and added meaning to text elements. This applies to the colours printed and the substrate upon which they are reproduced. The ability of foil to pick up and reflect colours around it can also be used to add dynamism to typographical elements.

In typography, colour can also describe the balance between black and white on a page of text. As different typefaces have different stroke widths, x-heights and serif styles, fonts set in the same size, with the same leading and other dimensions will produce varying degrees of 'colour' coverage on the page, and give the impression of different colours. Although this is an extreme example, it illustrates the point well. Slab serif font Aachen has broad strokes and appears very black on the page as the ink dominates.

In contrast, Helvetica 25 has fine, delicate lines that appear much lighter. As there is less ink on the page, the white stock dominates and gives the page a grey 'colour'. Cheltenham is stockier and has a lower x-height than Helvetica. While not as 'black' as Aachen, it creates the impression of a condensed black line crossing the page, as does Times New Roman and Perpetua, to a lesser degree.

Specifying colour

Most desktop publishing programs allow type to be specified according to different colour systems, notably Pantone and Hexachrome. When preparing work for on-screen use, designers employ the RGB (red, green and blue) colour selection, and when preparing for print they use CMYK (cyan, magenta, yellow and black).

100% M 100% Y	100% C 100% Y	100% C 100% M	70% C 60% M 70% Y 40% K	6% C 12% M 5% Y

High values of two colours give a strong, definite colour. High aggregate values result in a muddy colour. Low value tints can cause visible dot gain.

Colour associations

There are thousands of colours to choose from but it is important to highlight that certain colours are associated with particular meanings. For example, red is used in China for weddings and funerals because it represents celebration and luck. The same colour in Eastern cultures represents joy, while in Western cultures it represents danger. Blue is a sacred colour for Hindus as it is the colour of Krishna. It is also a holy colour in the Jewish faith, while the Chinese link blue to immortality. In Western culture, white is a colour of purity used for weddings, but in Eastern cultures it is a colour of mourning, symbolizing death.

This poster was created by George & Vera design studio for an exhibition for artist Kate Davis at London's Fred gallery. George & Vera used a simple typographic layout and different coloured inks with elements from Davis's 'Condition' series of drawings, which covers the changing moods and sentiments we associate with colours.

Surprint, overprint, knockout and reverse

These terms relate to how printing inks can produce different effects. A surprint uses tints of the same colour to create texture. An overprint occurs when one ink is applied over another, usually a darker ink is printed over a lighter one. Knockout printing is a gap left in the base colour, allowing other colours, an image or the unprinted page to show through. In contrast, a reverse sees one colour printing out of another – not allowing any other element to show through.

The panels above show how the order and settings of elements can create different effects. A surprint features tints of the same colour, in this case black. In an overprint, one ink is applied over another – with no gap left in the base colour. A knockout shows a gap left in the base colour whereas reverse printing sees one colour printing out of another, in this case yellow printing out of black.

The word 'overprint' is printed twice (above) using the four CMYK process colours. The left set is overprint while the right set is knockout. Overprinting effectively blends the printed colours to produce new ones such as green, while knocking out retains the purity of the individual colours. These techniques give a designer options for graphic manipulation by extending the range of the colour palette used, without the need to use different printing inks.

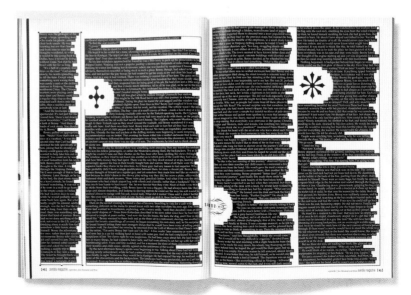

Above

This spread from *Juice* magazine created by
Parent design studio features an overprint over
a photo on the verso page, with text reversed
out of a solid colour on the recto page.

Right

Spread from the magazine *Zembla* created by
design studio Frost design. A knockout out was
used to create a white on black tapestry of type.

Printing and type realization

The way text elements are presented in a design is not just a
question of font selection, styling and positioning within a piece.
As the examples on this spread illustrate, the printing method to be
used and whether any print finishing will be required are important
post-design considerations. A design undergoes a metamorphosis from
what is created on screen to the production of the final product.

The examples on this page are intended to give an overview of the possibilities of type
realization. Many final printed pieces involve several of these processes, and the art of
combining them can create some sensational, dynamic and brave work. Common to all
is that they add to perceived value and enable work to appear unique and unusual.

Letterpress

Webb & Webb used
letterpress to give this
showreel packaging for
photographer Robert Dowling
a bespoke touch. Letterpress
prints differently according to
the amount of ink and pressure
on the printing press, giving
work an individual twist.

Hot metal type

The cover of *Paw Prints*, a self-
published book produced by
design studio Webb & Webb,
features letterpress typography
on a duplexed cover substrate
that is a combination of paper
board and endpapers. Hot metal
type gives a tactile impression to
the page.

Gravure

Gravure is a high-volume
intaglio printing process in
which the printing area is
etched into the printing plate,
and is capable of fine detail and
reliable results. This example is
from *1000 years 1000 words*, a
book designed by Webb & Webb
for Royal Mail, UK.

Silk screen

This invitation for Staverton
furniture by SEA Design has
the text screen printed in white
on blocks of yellow perspex in
order to create a distinctive and
weighty invitation. Silk
screening allows almost any
substrate to be printed.

Fluorescents and specials

Pictured is a book with metallic type, designed by Still Waters Run Deep. Special colours also include pastels, metallics and fluorescents, which are printed via a separate pass and give rich, vibrant colours. Special colours are also flat, containing no dots, as they are not made from CMYK process colours.

Spot UV

The cover of this brochure created for property developer Austin Gray by Parent design studio features a dual line font printed in a spot UV varnish. Spot UV varnishes are striking and heavy. Not only can they be seen on the page, they can also be felt as a raised surface.

Thermography

A method of applying a powder to a still-wet printed sheet, which is then heated, leaving a mottled texture. This Christmas card for Lisa Pritchard Agency by SEA Design was thermographically printed leaving 'bubbly' characters that are highly visible, tactile and reflect light in a unique way.

Varnish

This invitation, designed by Turnbull Grey for risk specialist Marsh Mercer, features text reversed out of a pearlescent varnish that can only be read when it catches the light. Several varnishes are available to choose from including gloss, matt, satin and more adventurous ones such as pearlescent.

Emboss

This brochure cover designed by Faydherbe / De Vringer features an embossed title to give added depth. In an emboss a pair of dies are used to raise the surface of the substrate. An emboss is usually applied with ink or a foil. A blind emboss occurs when no ink is applied.

Deboss

This brochure by Faydherbe / De Vringer features debossed typography covered with a UV lacquer. A deboss uses a pair of dies to make a deep impression in the printed surface. A blind emboss uses no ink or foil, whereas a deboss is usually applied with colour.

Die cut

This invitation by Studio Myerscough features die-cut text, giving a textural quality to the piece. Die cuts are usually applied after printing. Laser-cutting gives a more accurate cut, but is more expensive.

Foil blocking

This business card was created for interior designers d-raw Associates by MadeThought and features silver-foil type that has been stamped into light-coloured greyboard. Foils are available in many textures and colours, and can add a reflective dimension to a piece of work.

Above

This book for the Asian Development Bank called *'Reflections & Beyond'* was designed by Webb & Webb and uses letterpress typography. The book celebrates 25 years of the bank and is a series of 'verbal histories' of the staff.

Right and above right

The type, set by printers Hand & Eye, features a series of 'images'. For example the Manila skyline, shown right, which accompanies personal stories from people living in the Philippines. The rotated 'J' shown on the spread above represents a new water infrastructure project that the bank supports.

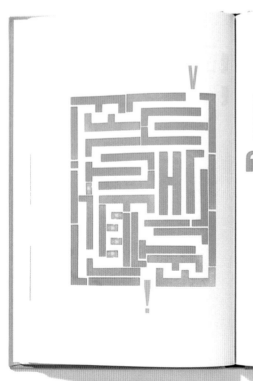

Above left and left

Letters form a suitcase, representing workers arriving, while a maze of letters illustrates the chapter opener 'Complex Situations and Tricky Judgement Calls'.

Above

An accompanying CD containing sounds and stories from the region was also printed in letterpress.

Duplexing
Bespoke and Window Envelopes
C6/DL Envelopes
Embossing
Cut Sizes
25 Sheet Minimum Order
Dummy Service
Sample and Advisory Service

Hull
GF Smith
Lockwood Street
Hull HU2 0HL

Telephone
01482 323 503
Facsimile
01482 223 174
Email
info@gfsmith.com

www.gfsmith.com

London
GF Smith
2 Leathermarket
Weston Street
London SE1 3ET

Telephone
020 7407 6174
Facsimile
020 7403 1037
Email
london@gfsmith.com

C6 Envelope

Part of GF Smith
Factory Services

This is a machine made C6 wallet style envelope with a peel and seal flap.
Made from Colorplan Scarlet 135gsm with a Brocade embossing.
The flat sheets of Colorplan have been foil blocked with a gold metallic
foil and then converted into envelopes by GF Smith. Minimum 500 envelopes.

Opposite

This is the Yearling *Jazz & Classics* direct mailer created for Arjo Wiggins by Thomas Manss & Co. design studio. The qualities of the paper are articulated through a series of specialist printing techniques. Here they have used letterpress and a bronze foil. Typographical elements are used in images to mimic details of musical instruments.

Above

This envelope was created by design studio SEA Design for paper merchant GF Smith to demonstrate the quality and flexibility of the stock, and showcase the creative use of colour. The scarlet base stock has a brocade emboss and gold foil block to exaggerate the decadent patterning.

Type on screen

The use of type on screen shares many of the requirements and concerns of type on a printed page. The same thought patterns govern the use of layout and the font choices made, but the end result is a little less controllable.

HTML vs Flash

When designing for screen, an important factor for consideration is whether the design will be built using HTML or Flash. Both have advantages and disadvantages and designers and clients need to be clear about the intentions of a website from the outset. HTML is a progamming language, and creates websites where the content is easily searchable by search engines. Flash on the other hand isn't easy to search, and isn't as easy to update as HTML. Blogs, forums and social networking sites are easier to integrate into a HTML site, and this will undoubtedly have an impact on the route people choose to take. The main advantage of Flash is that a designer has greater control over what a web page will look like over a series of different machines. HTML, in contrast, will look different on different machines – though it is worth remembering that this also means that users with special needs and requirements will also be better catered for.

Left

Shown here is a website and its hand-held device version, by Creasence Design for *Far From Moscow*. The site is a resource for promoting and recording emerging music from Russia, Ukraine, and Belarus, together with the Baltic nations (Latvia, Lithuania, Estonia). The site is edited and updated by David MacFadyen (Department of Slavic Languages and Literatures at the University of California, Los Angeles). The site embraces the new technology offered by the web, and uses a simple, clear, hierarchical typography style.

Standard fonts for use on PCs have Macintosh equivalents that are designed to fulfil the same tasks. For example, there are standard serif and sans serif fonts, a cursive font and so on as illustrated in the lists below. These standard fonts and their counterparts have the same set widths, as the two passages of text set in Century Gothic and Avant Garde show.

Standard PC fonts	Standard Macintosh fonts
Century Gothic	Avant Garde
Arial	Helvetica
Arial Narrow	Helvetica Narrow
Times New Roman	Times Roman
New Courier	Courier
Century Schoolbook	New Century Schoolbook
Bookman Old Style	ITC Bookman
Monotype Corsiva	*Zapf Chancery*
Monotype Sorts	ITC Zapf Dingbats
Symbol	Symbol
Σψμβολ	Σψμβολ

Fonts have equivalents which mean that the space they occupy on a web page is identical when viewed using different operating systems, although the font may appear different. The use of equivalents prevents text from being reflowed when displayed on different platforms. The two lists above show various fonts and their equivalents. This is Century Gothic, the PC equivalent of ITC Avant Garde (right).

Fonts have equivalents which mean that the space they occupy on a web page is identical when viewed using different operating systems, although the font may appear different. The use of equivalents prevents text from being reflowed when displayed on different platforms. The two lists above show various fonts and their equivalents. This is ITC Avant Garde, the Mac equivalent of Century Gothic (left).

145

Before

After

This identity and website design by Creasence Design shows the translation of traditional design skills into online activity. A clear hierarchy, a refined colour palette and controlled, restrained typography creates a sense of order, while still feeling feminine and inviting. You'll also notice over a series of pages from the website, that layout and alignment are used to create pace and structure.

As part of the redesign, the original logo, shown above left, was refined and simplified for use online. The original logo is unnecessarily confused and cluttered, and the revised identity brings a sense of care and structure to the design.

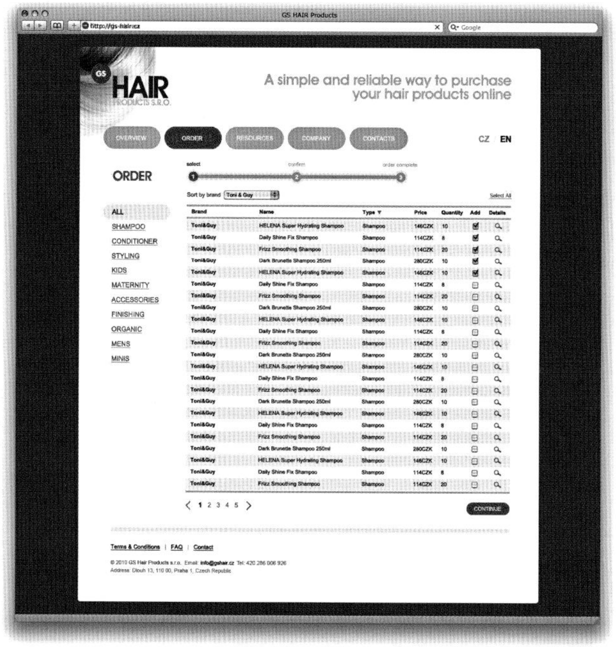
GS HAIR Products
HAIR
PRODUCTS S.R.O.
A simple and reliable way to purchase
your hair products online
OVERVIEW
ORDER
RESOURCES
COMPANY
CONTACTS
CZ EN
ORDER
ALL
SHAMPOO
CONDITIONER
STYLING
KIDS
MATERNITY
ACCESSORIES
FINISHING
ORGANIC
MENS
MINIS
CONTINUE

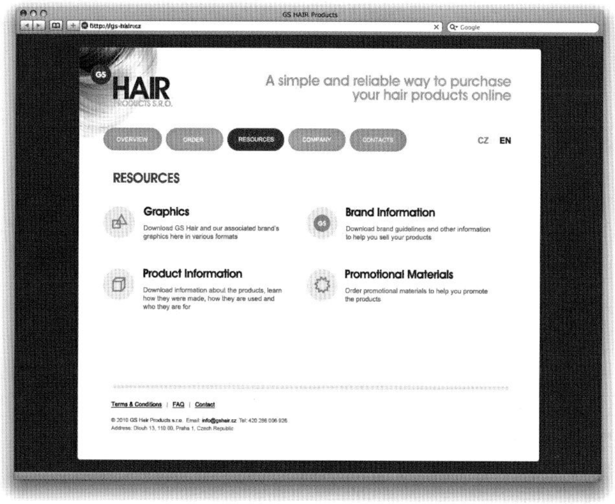
GS HAIR Products
HAIR
A simple and reliable way to purchase
your hair products online
CZ EN
RESOURCES
Graphics
Brand Information
Product Information
Promotional Materials

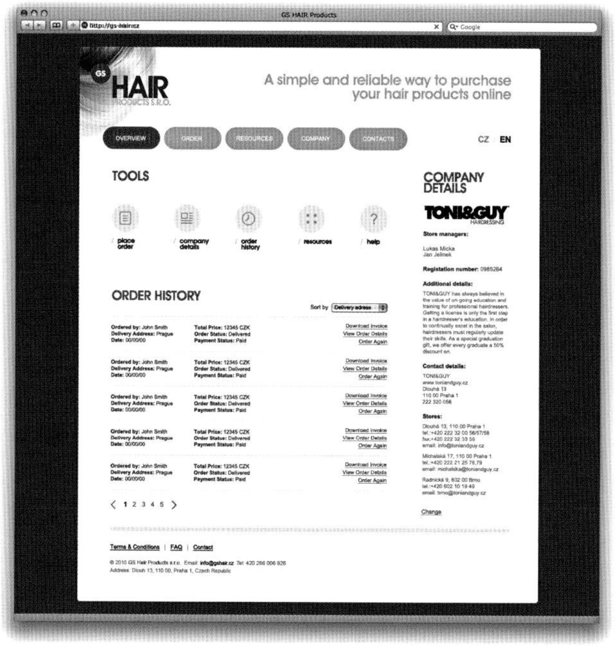
GS HAIR Products
HAIR
A simple and reliable way to purchase
your hair products online
CZ EN
TOOLS
COMPANY DETAILS
TONI&GUY
ORDER HISTORY

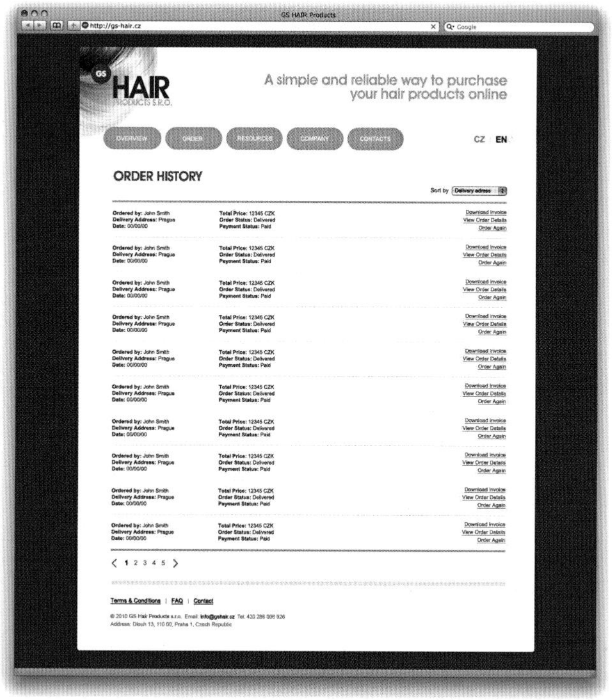
GS HAIR Products
HAIR
A simple and reliable way to purchase
your hair products online
CZ EN
ORDER HISTORY

Grids and fonts

Grids can be used as a basis for creating typography, with the letterforms built around the structure of a grid rather than being penned by hand or based on carved letterforms like traditional typographic forms.

ABCDEFGHIJKLMNOPQRSTUVWXYZ
abcdefghijklmnopqrstuvwxyz 1234567890

Foundry Gridnik Light
Often described as the thinking man's Courier, Foundry Gridnik is based on a font by Dutch designer Wim Crouwel, and takes its name from his devotion to the grid – he was often called 'Mr Gridnik' by his contemporaries in the 1960s.

ABCDEFGHIJKLMNOPQRSTUVWXYZ
abcdefghijklmnopqrstuvwxyz
1234567890

OCR-B
The OCR-B font was designed as an optical character recognition font (OCR) and as such can be scanned and turned back into editable text. To aid this process the characters are made additionally explicit to avoid any confusion, which would lead to scrambled text. The capital 'I' for example has exaggerated slab serifs so that it cannot be confused with the number '1'. The capital 'O' is very round in comparison to the number '0', again to prevent confusion. This is a monospaced font which means that all characters, however thin, occupy the same amount of space.

ABCDEFGHIJKLMNOPQRSTUVWXYZ
abcdefghijklmnopqrstuvwxyz1234567890

Data Seventy
Data Seventy is reminiscent of LED calculator display screens from the 1970s. The characters appear very square and have a space-age feel.

This is Moonbase Alpha, created by Swiss typographer Cornel Windlin in 1991 for issue 3 of font magazine FUSE, which focused on disinformation. Windlin used type generation software for the first time in the design, which was based on a pixelated printout of 4pt Akzidenz Grotesk that he cleaned up, restructured and partly redesigned.

Generating type

While there are thousands of typefaces available, it is sometimes necessary to generate new ones. Fonts can be produced in a number of different ways, from creating original art to replicating type from older publications, mark making or rendering type in font generation programs. The ability to create fonts electronically has enabled fonts to be generated quickly, in response to the specific needs and desires of clients, designers and typographers.

FF Stealth, above
FF Stealth has strong graphic presence. Created by Malcolm Garrett in 1995, it features minimalist forms reminiscent of occult symbols.

FF Karton, above
Designed by Just van Rossum in 1992, this font has the appearance of being *sprayed*, rather than printed.

This is an identity created by Studio Myerscough for webwizards. It uses a typeface inspired by the Slinky toy. The letters replicate the movements of a Slinky's coils.

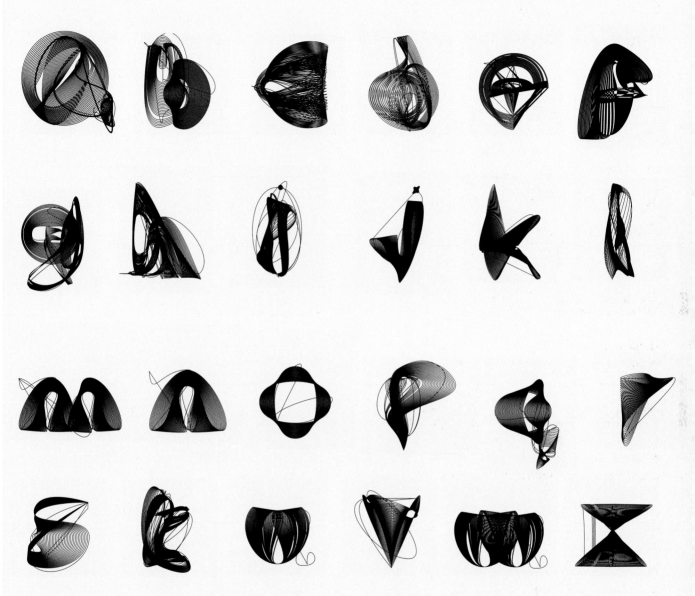

This typeface was created by London design studio Research Studios to promote 'Made in Clerkenwell', an open event held in central London. To reflect the precise and crafted, artisan-nature of the works exhibited (including ceramics, textiles and jewellery), a hand-drawn type was developed. The typeface was generated using vector paths, as these can be quickly manipulated to obtain the desired shape and style for each letter. Each character is created using lines of the same width, ensuring consistency and a degree of uniformity from letter to letter.

A masthead design by Planning Unit that makes reference to op art. The logo is deceptively simple, while also being amazingly complicated. The illusion of movement is created by the expressive lines that collide to make letters, as though shimmering in a pool of water.

Vectors and rasters

There are essentially two ways of digitally storing typography: in vector format and in raster format. Each has its own advantages and disadvantages, and there are instances where both will be used on a single job, as shown on the following spread.

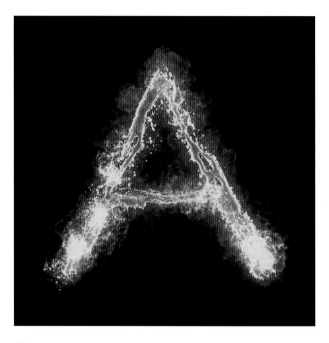

Vectors

Nearly all fonts are saved as vector-based information. That is to say that they are constructed from a set of mathematical coordinates and values, which in turn generate the typefaces we use. For this reason they can be resized at will, and can be enlarged indefinitely, without any degradation in quality or loss of sharpness. This means they can be easily distributed, and you only need the main font file to be able to generate text at any size. The limitation is that they tend to be constructed from crisp, linear lines, and it can be hard to assimilate texture, or any graphic effects while in a vector format.

Rasters

Once type is rasterized (that is to say converted from lines and coordiantes into pixels, like a photographic image) any number of effects and styles can be applied. This is usually only done for titles, and for on-screen work, such as title sequences in a film. The disadvantage of this approach is that once converted into a raster format, type is no longer editable as letters and words, as it is now essentially a picture made of pixels and colour information. You also need to be aware that rasters are of a finite size and can't be enlarged without degradation of image quality.

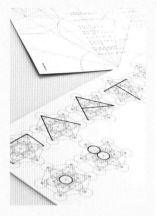

Above and right

Shown is a poster and invitation
to a concert by pianist and
composer Lena Platonos by The
Design Shop. The typography is
based on the symbol for the
'Fruit of Life'. The Fruit of Life
is a geometrical figure, said to
be the blueprint for the universe,
based on 13 circles. The shape
shown here is called Metaton's
Cube, and within this,
typographical forms are set.
The accuracy of vector graphics
is used to create the detailed line
work and geometric forms.

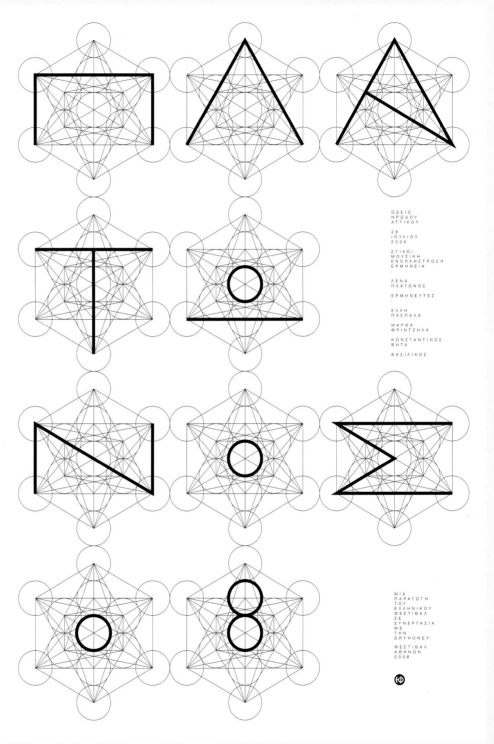

THINGS TO DO BEFORE YOU LEAVE TOWN

ROSS SUTHERLAND

Rẽx

Napoleon's Travelling Bookshelf

Sarah Hesketh

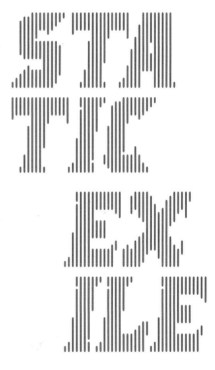

This page and opposite

Generation Txt is a series of books published by Penned in the Margins and designed by the design and arts collective, Mercy. The books demonstrate an eclectic range of approaches to typography and the complex relationship between text and image. From type-set forms to hand-rendered marks, the resulting covers are both dynamic and engaging. The various book titles are a mixture of vector and raster graphics. On the page opposite, 'Napoleon's Travelling Bookcase' uses a raster artwork to get texture and degradation, while in contrast, 'Static Exile' (right) makes use of vector artwork to generate a clean, accurate design.

Legibility and readability

These two terms are often used synonymously. Strictly speaking, *legibility* refers to the ability to distinguish one letterform from another through the physical characteristics inherent in a particular typeface, such as x-height, character shapes, counter size, stroke contrast and type weight. *Readability* concerns the properties of a piece of type or design that affect the ability to make it understood. That is to say that you don't need to be able to *read* something, to *understand* it. Graffiti that is illegible allows people to read anger on the part of the protagonist, for example.

Ab

The decorative nature of the Benguiat font means that when set as body copy it can be hard to read, as the decorative elements impede the eye tracking across the text and break the reading flow. While characters at display size are clear, at smaller sizes legibility is compromised.

Ab

In contrast to the example above, Ionic is designed specifically for newspaper applications; its exaggerated serifs, large open counters and relatively large x-height means that it is easy to read over extended texts.

abcdefghijklmnopqrstuvwxyz

ABCDEFGHIJKLMNOPQRSTUVWXYZ

ABCDEFGHIJKLMNOPQRSTUVWXYZ

The fonts above (from top to bottom: Crash, Caustic Biomorph Extra Bold and Barnbrook Gothic Three) may not be the most legible, but in the right contexts they can inform the reader through their readability - character forms themselves convey an instant message in addition to the words they spell.

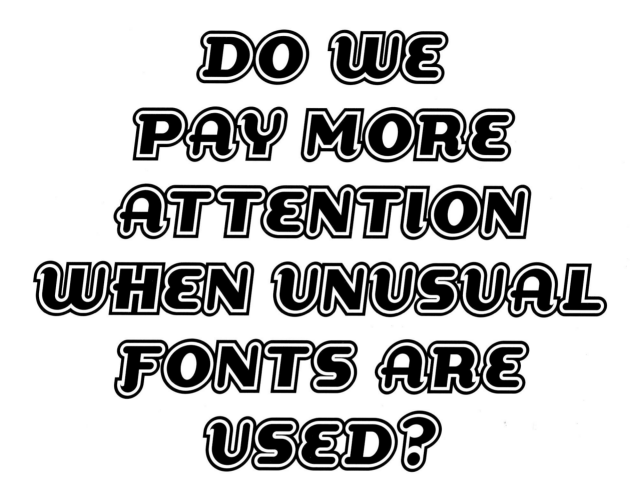

DO WE PAY MORE ATTENTION WHEN UNUSUAL FONTS ARE USED?

Emerging research shows that we actually learn better when the learning is made harder. This sounds counter-intuitive, but using fonts that require more effort to read can actually force the brain to interpret the information in a different way. Neuroscientist Jonah Lehrer explains: *'When we see a font that is easy to read, something like Helvetica, we are able to process it in a very mindless way. But when we see an unfamiliar font, a font full of weird squiggles and curlicues, the visual cortex in the brain has to work a little bit harder and the extra effort is a signal to the brain that this is worth remembering.'* Although this may sound odd, how many times do we see type set in the same few fonts? *Helvetica*, *Times* and *Arial* are so familiar that it

could be argued that they, and any message they carry, will simply wash over us. Fonts less frequently seen, such as *Dogma*, as shown above, could possibly be unusual enough to encourage the reader to stop, read and remember. Lehrer continues: *'When the part of our brain devoted to reading has to exert that extra bit of effort we may actually remember what we are reading even better.'*

Texture

Typography is just one element of a design, used in combination with images, diagrams, photography and other graphic elements. Type forms part of a larger visual scheme. The vast array of typefaces available means that type can be used to add a great deal of texture to a design, as the examples in this spread show.

ABCDEFGHIJKLMNOPQRSTUVWXYZ

ABCDEFGHIJKLMNOPQRSTUVWXYZ

ABCDEFGHIJKLMNOPQRSTUVWXYZ

The fonts above (from top: Stamp Gothic, Confidential and Flight Case) show how texture can be added to a typeface design. The fonts offer a facsimile of the patchy nature of other printing methods and are used to add an effect of degradation.

Left

This cover was created by design studio Frost Design and features a single letterpressed ampersand character at a monumental scale. The inherent texture of the process creates interest and a point of difference.

Opposite

Texture has been added to this identity for an art gallery on the island of Kea, Greece, by infilling the counters of the letters, creating a strong visual pattern. The design, by The Design Shop, is intended to 'combine the dynamic but simple aesthetics of a contemporary art space, with the feeling of the island landscape'.

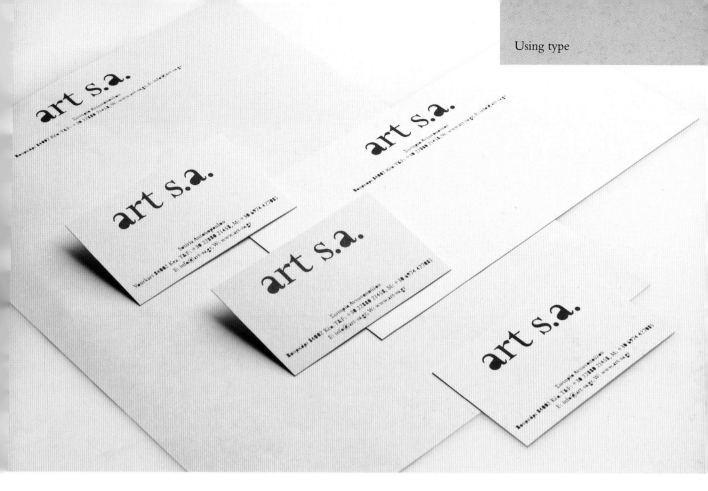

apples to books to comics
[ ] decoration to earrings to
fl uffy clouds to giraffes to
h ndbags to ideas to jigsaws
t [kaleidoscopes to loving
t [mornings to notebooks to
c riginality to prints to questions
t [rainbows to soaps to time
[ ] umbrellas to vices to wonders
[ ] x-static to you to zebras

Above

In this identity The Design Shop added texture by choosing the right words. Apples to Zebras sell a range of eclectic gifts, and this identity is all about selecting and editing. As Mark Twain said: 'The difference between the almost-right word and the right word is the difference between the lightning bug and the lightning!'

PLUG ///// ///

A / NEW / ////

A/NEW/VENUE/IN/SHEFFIELD/3/ROOMS/LIVE/EARTH/NEUTRAL/////////////

PLUG/FRIDAYS
7TH/OCTOBER///////////////////   14TH/OCTOBER////////////////////
JEFF/MILLS//////////////////   PETE/TONG////////////////////
X-ECUTIONERS//FIRST/RATE//////   BENJI/B////////////////////

PLUG/SATURDAYS
8TH/OCTOBER///////////////////   15TH/OCTOBER////////////////////
TIM/DELUXE//////////////////   NASTY/DIRTY/SEX/MUSIC//////////
CJ/MACINTOSH//////////////////   CARIBOU/(LIVE)////////////////

LIVE/MUSIC
4TH/OCTOBER////THE/EDITORS//////////////////////////
15TH/OCTOBER///ARCTIC/MONKEYS///////////////////////
17TH/OCTOBER///LADYTRON/////////////////////////////
22ND/OCTOBER///TOM/VEK//////////////////////////////
31ST/OCTOBER///FOUR/TET//SUPPORT/EXPLOSIONS/IN/THE/SKY//////////

3RD/NOVEMBER///JAMIE/LIDDELL//SUPPORT/JACKSON///////////////////
6TH/NOVEMBER///MARTHA/WAINWRIGHT///////////////////////////////

FOR/INFORMATION/OR/TO/MAKE/BOOKINGS/VISIT////////////////////
WWW.TICKETWEB.CO.UK//OR/TELEPHONE/08700/600100///////////////
TELEPHONE//0114/2762676//WWW.THE-PLUG.COM//INFO@THE-PLUG.COM////
PLUG//14-16//MATILDA//STREET//SHEFFIELD//S1//4QD//////////////

plug

TICKETWEB·
www.ticketweb.co.uk

BROWN/IS/LIVE
BLUE/IS/NEUTRAL

Left and below
Peter and Paul design studio
added texture to these designs
by overprinting type on the
base image and subtly layering
information.

Type as image

In addition to spelling out words, type is also used as a graphic device that speaks more through its visual representation than the meanings of the constituent letters.

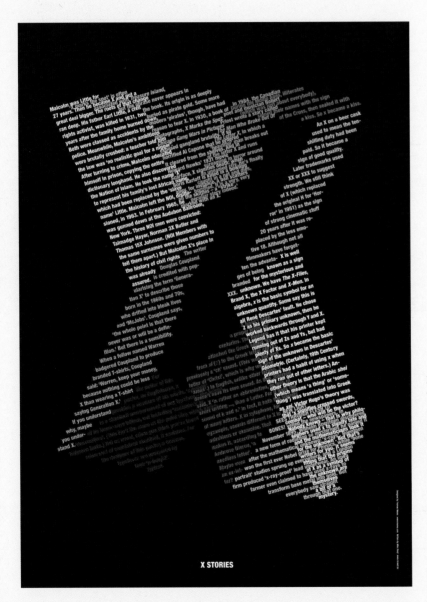

X STORIES

Left

This poster was part of the '26 Letters: Illuminating the Alphabet' poster series for an exhibition at the British Library in London, developed and curated by 26, who promote writing in business, and the International Society of Typographic Designers. Thomas Manss, of Thomas Manss & Co., and writer Mike Reed created X using ten stories featuring the letter (including the discovery of x-rays, how Malcolm X got his name and Robert Priest's short story, *The Man Who Broke Out of the Letter X*). The artwork features a rainbow-coloured, three-dimensional 'X' constructed from passages of the stories.

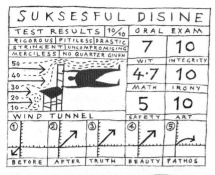

THIS IS NOT A CHAIR

Oak from the Von der Borch estate forest Westfalia GR
Some thanks to Antoine

SAFETY INSTRUCTIONS
1. Most of the component must fit into the board in correct direction. In some of these cases the components are marked accordingly. The hinges are neither marked by means of coloured rings nor direct labelling. In case of many small miniature components it is difficult to recognise the colour code or labelling. We therefore recommend to check value of resistor before filling.
2. Usually a holder for the IC is attached. If necessary the connecting pins have to be bent a bit (with a small pair of pliers) For this purpose a narrow side of the case is marked; with a notch, a point impression, a deepened triangle or something like that. In rare cases the vertical is not marked at all.
3. These products do not have any CE acceptance. May contain substances which are harmful to the body. Dangerous situations may occur during starting when making a mistake (e.g. cables may glow or catch fire) The presence of a competant person is always necessary during mounting. If the module or device does not work properly, accidents happened (liquid ran into the device, device fell down etc.) or if it causes strange noises or smells, switch off immediately. Ask an expert for examination.
4. BORCH/FISHER disclaim any responsibility for anything they have done in the past or anything they might do in the future.

Above and right

All the handwritten type in this brochure was created by Webb & Webb design studio for an exhibition of chairs by Nicholas Von der Borch and Jeff Fisher. The result is a mix of words, drawn symbols, sketches and mis-spellings (such as 'suksesful disine'), which creates a strong, image-based visual impression. It also tips its hat to a surrealist painting by René Magritte *Ceci n'est pas une pipe* ('This is not a pipe').

2½ dimensions. We are chair 🚶🚶🪑 Why the bottom is so important Comfort leads to idleness. GOOD POSTURE leads 🪑🪑 to glory. Comfort 👓🚲 is an illusion. You never relax in a good chair. Ⓑ Ⓕ devote their lives to this. 🪑→🪑 Start from a drawing of a

chair, extrapolate into a 3D object. 🪑 The result is a sculpture of a drawing. Ⓑ Ⓕ look at the chair from 2½ directions, 👓👓 & impossibly, have reinvented the chair. The middle ground between 2D & 3D is a landscape Ⓑ Ⓕ will ultimately widen to encompass everything. Nicholas Von der Borch & Jeff Fisher are chair.

165

Concrete poetry, typograms, trompe l'œil and calligrammes

Text can have a playful side – and these common 'tricks' can add interest to a design. If used correctly, these approaches can create subtle and effective additions to a typographer's arsenal.

Concrete poetry

Concrete poetry is experimental poetry from the 1950-1960s that concentrated on the visual appearance of words through the use of different typographical arrangements, such as the use of shaped text blocks and collage. The intent of the poet is conveyed by the shape the poem takes rather than a conventional reading of the words. As concrete poetry is visual, its effect is lost when a poem is read aloud.

Typograms

A typogram refers to the deliberate use of typography to express an idea visually, but by incorporating something more than just the letters that constitute the word. For example, the word 'half' cut in half and displayed with only half visible letters would be a typogram.

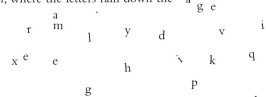

Meaning 'trick of the eye' a *trompe l'œil* is an optical illusion in which a design is made to look like something it is not. Common *trompe l'œil* tricks include making type appear as if it is an object, applied to the page, or 'stuck-on'.

Calligramme

French writer Guillaume Apollinaire invented calligrammes in 1918, which he described as 'painting with words'. From the Greek, *callos*, meaning 'beauty', and *gram/graph*, meaning 'written' or 'write', a calligramme is a word, phrase or poem that is written so that it forms an image of the subject of the text. A famous calligramme is *Il pleut*, where the letters rain down the page.

Above

This book was created by Cartlidge Levene design studio for an exhibition of the work of sound installation artist Bruce Nauman at London's Tate Modern Gallery. The book features spreads that are set with type patterns referring to his works, in an attempt to visually convey with static text the playfulness of the sounds in his works and their aural repetition.

HO
HO

Above and following page
Pictured above and on the
following page is the cover and
inside of an invitation created
by Webb & Webb design studio
for an event at Hogarth's House
in London. To convey a sense
of the festivities, the name of
the institution is split or
wrapped around from the
cover to the inner to produce
the jolly 'Ho Ho' typogram.

Above

This is a poster created for an architecture exhibition by Chilean design studio Y&R. It features
a capital 'A' drawn like a solid structure, representing architecture. The crossbar in the form of an
eye refers to the fact that at an exhibition a visitor looks at things.

GARTH'S
USE

Sir Peter Blake and the William Hogarth Trust

invite you to a celebration at

Hogarth's House, Hogarth Lane, Great West Road, London W4
on Thursday 27 May, 6.30-8.30pm
to mark the centenary of its opening as a museum.

We would be delighted if you were able to join us

RSVP
William Hogarth Trust
telephone/answerphone/fax 020 8995 9013
8 Heathfield Gardens, London W4 4JY

Registered Charity no 1092251

Left
See previous page.

Below
This logo by Thomas Manss &
Co. for Metamorphosis hints at
the transformation of a
caterpillar to a butterfly.

Right
This poster was created by
Angus Hyland at Pentagram for
the London College of Printing
to promote an exhibition of
logos created by the design
studio. The word 'Symbol' has
been turned into a logotype to
illustrate the nature of what
logotypes can become.

Symbol™

Humour

We tend to think of typography as being a serious subject, concerned with detail, measurements and relationships, and to a certain extent it is. But typography also has a unique place in our lives, we interact with it in so many different ways. Humour is often employed as a persuasion technique in advertising and design, and can be subtle and sophisticated, as the examples on this spread demonstrate.

Above
This invitation was created by Turnbull Grey design studio for private equity firm Bain & Company. The ascenders have been extended to appear like drinking straws. This shows how type can be constantly altered, and new meanings formed. It is also a reminder that type is there to inform, but it can also amuse and entertain.

Right
This is the cover of a property brochure created by Studio Myerscough design studio for the *Sweeps Building* development in Clerkenwell, London. It features hand-drawn script letterforms reflecting the name of the development.

design:

Above and right

This identity by Mouse Graphics for the body responsible for promoting Greek design abroad makes use of the 'hidden' 'gr' (for Greece) in the word design. This makes a statement about Greece becoming a more prominent force in modern graphic design. This is an example of a two-in-one, a common form of typographic humour, where two messages are conveyed in a single unit.

Environmental typography

Type can be larger than life, adopting a physical presence in the environment, as the examples on this spread show.

Left
This signage at London Barbican was created by design studios Studio Myerscough and Cartlidge Levene. The large-scale signage wraps around the building like a second skin, with apertures cut away that allow the building to show through.

Above
The DIN-Schrift typeface is used on German road signage. As this is often reversed out of black and viewed in poor conditions, the letterforms have been tweaked to add clarity. For example, the counter of the 'o' has been made more oval, letters have been lengthened, and the umlaut diacritical mark has been made circular rather than square.

The images above show the original typeface and how it looks in poor visibility (left) and the enhanced typeface and how it looks in poor visibility (above).

Above

This installation was created by Gavin Ambrose for the Design Council to reduce complex statistical information to single 'facts' that invite the viewer to interact with them. The explanation or significance of each number is screen printed on the side of its constructed form and viewers are actively encouraged to sit on and explore the letterforms.

Left

This design by Studio Myerscough and architectural practice Allford Hall Monaghan Morris uses type at a large scale to indicate specific areas for children's activities such as netball, football and basketball. It is intended to be fun, engaging and ultimately informative.

Vernacular

Vernacular is the everyday language spoken by a group of people, including slang and regional phrasing. It is the language of the street, no matter where that street is. To a certain extent, the textures of vernacular can be communicated in text through the use of typography. Type has personality, and from the typographic choices made, text can be instilled with the personality of the typeface, whether conservative, authoritarian, young or rebellious.

Many fonts have a heritage that can be traced back to physical objects in the environment, some of which are shown below.

The Tape Type font utilizes the random patterns and irregular lines of packaging tape to create a clumsy and textured effect.

TAPE TYPE

Inspired by electronic display systems, the LED font is based on a simplified grid of seven bars.

LED

Stencil, created by Gerry Powell in 1938, looks industrial and durable, possibly mass produced or shipped from afar.

STENCIL

Crud font looks like a typewriter font that has been used extensively and has badly deteriorated.

Crud Font

This page
This signage at London's Tea Building was created by Studio Myerscough and features the simple beauty of a bespoke font. The rawness of the application is apt for the building, which contains many textures and exposed materials.

Appropriation

Appropriation is the borrowing of aesthetic elements from a particular epoch, style or movement and using them as part of another. Appropriated elements frequently have denotive and/or cognitive meanings that continue to function in their new role; placing them in a different historical context can subvert those meanings or the new context.

The new context can be so overwhelming that the original source of the appropriation is forgotten. Perhaps the most infamous example of this is the swastika. For 3,000 years it was a symbol of good luck and prosperity for societies including Hindus, Buddhists, Greeks, Romans, Aztecs, Persians and ancient Jewish peoples. Appropriated by Nazi Germany, it became a symbol of power and fear, representing the struggle for Aryan supremacy.

Left and below
These exhibition stands by Studio Myerscough demonstrate the power of appropriated typography. The bright show lights and glamour for the *Rock Style* exhibition appropriate the graphics and technology of the time.

Left

Type can occupy unexpected
places in the environment,
as this exhibition for Archigram
created by Studio Myerscough
design studio shows, with
deckchair canvas used as the
substrate. This appropriation
of one medium by another
demonstrates that you
shouldn't be limited in your
use of typography.

Ownership

Designs and typography can be so successful that they become inextricably linked to the products, organizations or events that they were created for. For this reason, many companies may consistently use the same font to enforce a sense of identity and ownership.

Times New Roman was designed for *The Times* newspaper by Stanley Morison and Victor Lardent and focused on expressing authoritative legibility.

Apple Macintosh uses a condensed Garamond in its marketing material, which strengthens Apple's relatively abstract logo to give logical consistency.

The Adidas brand is recognizable from the dynamic, geometric letterforms of Herb Lubalin's Avant Garde.

Confectionery brand M&M uses the distinctive slab serif Rockwell, which gives it a fun feel.

The titling on the Beach Boys 1966 album Pet Sounds used Cooper Black, forever linking it to the 1960s, though the typeface was actually created in 1921.

Futura, based on simple functional forms, has been used by German auto manufacturer Volkswagen since the 1960s. Paul Renner designed the original versions of Futura in 1927.

FASHION MAGAZINE *VOGUE* USES THE DISTINCTIVE AND ELEGANT BODONI LETTERFORMS, WHICH HAVE FINE SERIFS. BODONI IS NAMED AFTER GIAMBATTISTA BODONI, WHO DESIGNED IT IN 1798.

Absolut Vodka uses a condensed, extra bold version of Futura that results in an interesting contrast between x-height and ascender length.

Internet shopping website **amazon**.com uses Officina Sans (designed by Erik Spiekermann in 1990) in both bold and book for a no-nonsense look.

The London Underground uses Johnston's masterpiece sans serif typeface that bears his name. Johnston Underground also contains an extra set that features a range of symbols:

London Underground was later revisited and altered by Eric Gill. This revised form is used by clothing label Benetton, among others.

Above and left

The identity of branding and communications agency Osmosis has no definable logo. Instead, it features a series of 'O's in different typefaces that change with each application. This is part of a strategy to develop ownership of the letter over a period of time, as it becomes an intrinsic part of Osmosis' visual identity. Three-dimensional 'O's were created in a range of colours to be photographed in different environments and used on business cards and literature. Design agency Peter and Paul were tasked with the brief to 'create a visual identity bigger and deeper than a logo, colour, typeface and visual style; an identity that was individual, unique and memorable, that was inspiring, challenging and engaging. In short, "we want to own the letter 'O'".

The resulting design by Peter and Paul is both memorable, and successful, in that it does begin to take ownership of a letterform.

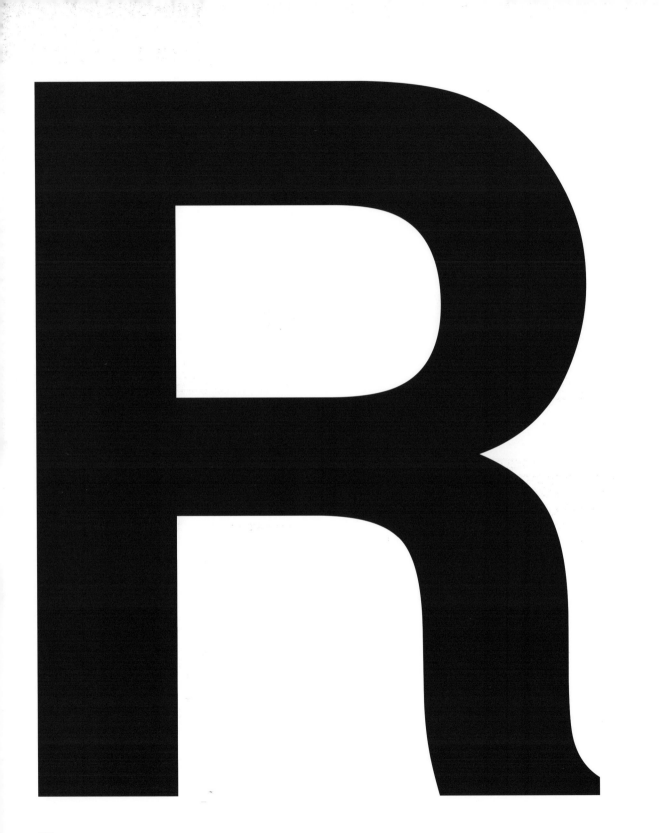

This page and opposite

This identity and packaging design for an experimental fashion label, by design agency Creasence, shows the power of using a simple element in a consistent manner. Taking ownership of the letter (the ubiquitous Helvetica 'R') or the colour (a straight Pantone Red), is always going to be hard, but by combining these elements the identity becomes distinct enough to become 'ownable'.

TRITON GLOBAL – WEBB & WEBB, UK

Project description

This identity by *Webb & Webb* for holding company *Triton* has been developed to reflect the nature of the businesses it contains. These professional indemnity and insurance law companies do not share the traditional formal image of solicitors and insurance brokers. The angular typography implies a slightly 'quirkier' nature to the business, while the rings formed by the converging 'o's imply evolution and change, and are also a reference to the global nature of the business.

In discussion with James Webb, of Webb & Webb

GA The identity features what one might call a 'gift', with the two words of the identity both containing a letter 'o', that enables you to make a connection, linguistically and visually. Do you look for these visual connections? Or is it a case of allowing them to surface? **JW** When we started working on Triton Global we needed to understand as much about the company (and companies) as we did about the nature of the job. Drawing a simple diagram (below) to show how the

several companies involved operate, both individually and with each other, not only helped us and the clients see how they operate but also formed a key part of the initial design process. The final outcome is a combination of several routes: the idea of 'global time' – that with several international offices, Triton would be at the centre; that one group company was both an individual specialist and also several parts of a whole; and a pictorial representation of the name (Triton being the largest orbiting moon of Neptune). Yes, the 'gift' works well and appears to be the most natural idea but it was only by working through all the other routes that we ended up with this.

GA The work of the studio could be said to have certain themes running through it. There is often a subtle sense of humour, and you often seem to find a particular quirk, or facet, that others may miss, like looking at a problem from a slightly different angle. When using typography do you have a particular approach or stance? The beauty of this project is that it manages to say two things in one, for example.

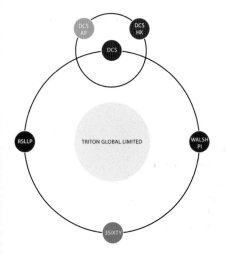

Left
Diagram showing the relative positions held by the range of companies the identity is trying to bring together.

Above
Experiments relating to the themes of time and the reference to the moon of Neptune, called Triton.

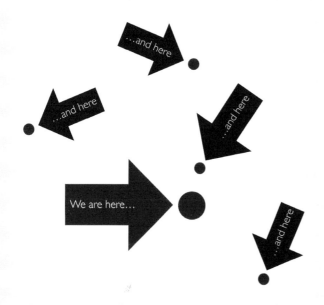

Above
Early 'positioning' of the brand.

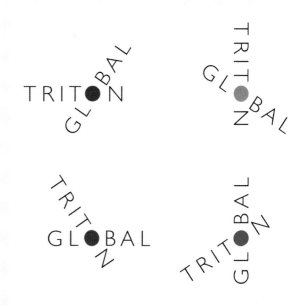

Above
Experiments in angles and convergence.

JW We really try to steer clear of an approach that could be called a studio style (although it is impossible not to be affected by current trends in art, design and even the political climate). Being communicators, we always try to put forward a clear message or idea within our work. When the project calls for it we might make the message deliberately difficult to work out!

GA How do you feel the choice of font here has had an influence on the design?
JW Our use of a particular font is influenced by the client or specific job – modern friendly communications need a look that reflects the message, for example. In this case I think it would be difficult to identify insurance specialists with a particular font and the choice is more about finding a typeface that has a visual harmony with the more complicated 'o' ring system. We used a slightly redrawn version of New Johnston, with a straight set of characters – finding a good R and G was important.

GA How did you develop the project typography into the final form? Is this a collaborative process in the studio, and did this process have much input from the client/s?

JW At the beginning of a project the whole studio will work on ideas, and the client will always have their favourite approach. In this instance they were keen on the idea behind the 'Global Time' approach but liked the 'crescent moon' shape in the pictorial approach so a combination of ideas by two designers was brought together into one identity. After that the application of the identity onto other items such as stationery, website, signage, etc. is usually put together by one person but we never stop asking within the studio group 'which works better?'.

GA There seems to be a snobbery in some typographic circles that certain typefaces or approaches can't be used. Does the studio have any rules, or feel constrained?
JW It's impossible not to have favourite fonts or typographic styles and working for a lot of our clients over long periods of time and on a multitude of different jobs means we get to learn their style or have to follow styles set by ourselves or other design companies. But we are never afraid to challenge the client with something new.

183

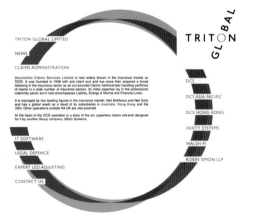

Above

The final typographic logo (above), and its expansion onto web (right) and moving image (top).

Thinking in words

Premise

Often, identities are created from 'hidden' details. An example is the Federal Express logo, which forms an arrow in the negative space where the 'E' and 'x' meet.

Others exploit the shape of words. For example, Baskin Robbins make 31 flavours of ice cream – this is cleverly highlighted in the stems of the 'B' and the 'R'. Oil company Mobil, uses the 'o' in its name to represent an oil pipe and wheel.

You can also make use of the sound of words – for example this identity for oil producer, Kuwait Petroleum International (Q8).

Sometimes, it is worth encouraging the viewer to work it out, in the form of a rebus, or puzzle – for example the ubiquitous *'I Love New York'* logo by Milton Glaser

Other common techniques include using *alliteration*, where the first syllable sound is repeated, such as in the computer games *Prince of Persia* and *Warrior Within*). *Substitution*, *addition* and *modification* are also common techniques of which *portmanteau* words are an example. In these word combinations, two or more words are used to create a new but linked word. Indeed, *FedEx* (shown opposite) is a portmanteau of 'Federal' and 'Express'. Many of these words have since come into common parlance, for example *blog* (web & log) or *brunch* (breakfast & lunch). Often, when these portmanteau words are brought together, the two original words are still identifiable, and are often marked by an upper-case letter. This technique of using an upper-case letter in the middle of a word is called *Camel Case* or *Inter Cap*. Although unconventional in normal prose, this approach has become relatively common in the creation of identities and brands.

Exercise

1. Select a company, real or fictitious, and simply using the characters of its name, experiment how it can be articulated using some or all of the devices described on this page.
2. Think about the pattern of the letters, the sound and the meaning. Does it have a pattern of ascenders and descenders, does it have a particular rhyming pattern, can you form a 'picture' out of any of the characters?
3. Consider how these effects can be used to enhance a logo or typographic marque.
4. Produce an identity/series of identities using these principles.

Outcome

To encourage experimental thinking in relation to words and sounds. To think about type in a new way.

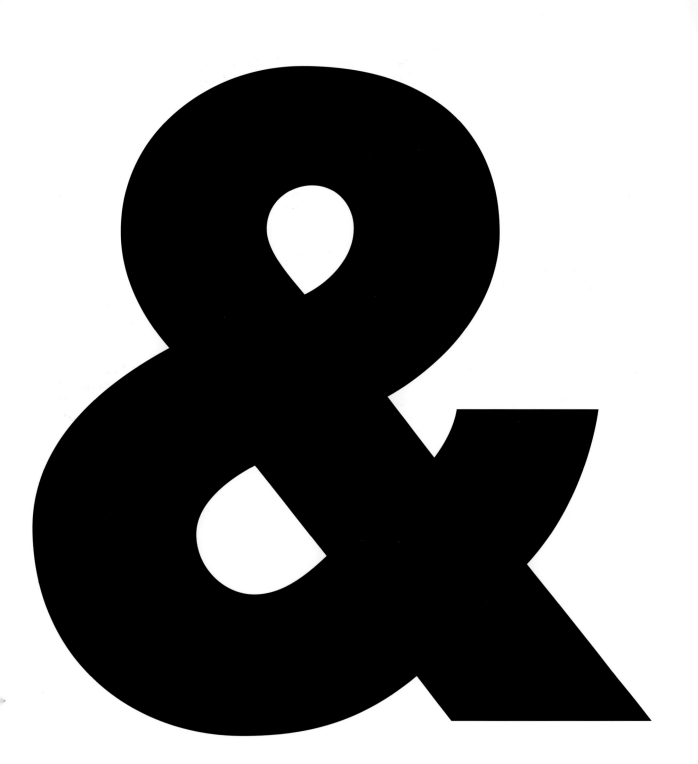

conclusion

Typography is an essential communication and design element that has evolved over several centuries, and continues to evolve as tastes change and technology makes it easier to develop new typefaces.

Type plays a fundamental role in the communication process as much through the shapes and styling of the letterforms as the actual words that they form.

This volume has attempted to outline the origins of type and show how it has developed through time to provide a base of information that can be used to inform typographical decision making. This volume has also attempted to show how type can be used creatively to enhance communication and produce visual impact, in addition to identifying key norms to guide type usage.

Typography can be a complex subject, with its own technical terms and jargon. These have been defined and explained to facilitate more precise communication of requirements.

We would like to thank everyone who has been involved in the production of this volume, especially all the designers and design studios that generously contributed examples of their work. And a final big thank you to Caroline Walmsley, Brian Morris and Leafy Robinson at AVA Publishing for all their help and support.

glossary

Apex
The point formed at the top of a character such as 'A' where the left and right strokes meet.

Bar
The horizontal stroke on characters 'A', 'H', 'T', 'e', 'f', 't'. Sometimes called a *crossbar* on 'A' and 'H' or arm on 'F', 'T', 'E' and 'K' upstroke.

Baseline
The baseline is an imaginary line upon which a line of text sits and is the point from which other elements of type are measured including *x-height* and *leading*.

Blackletter
A typeface based on the ornate writing prevalent during the Middle Ages. Also called block, gothic, old English, black or broken.

Body text
Body text or copy is the text that forms the main part of a work. It is usually between 8 and 14 *points* in size.

Bold
A version of the *Roman* with a wider *stroke*. Also called medium, semibold, black, super or poster.

Boldface type
A thick, heavy variety of type used to give emphasis.

Bowl
The *stroke* that surrounds and contains the *counter*.

Bracket
The curved portion of a *serif* that connects it to the *stroke*.

Character
An individual element of type such as a letter or punctuation mark.

Chin
The *terminal* angled part of the 'G'.

Condensed
A narrower version of the *Roman* cut.

Counter
The empty space inside the body stroke surrounded by the bowl.

Cross stroke
Horizontal stroke that crosses over the *stem*.

Crotch
Where the *leg* and *arm* of the 'K' and 'k' meet.

Cursive
Inclined *typeface* exhibiting calligraphic qualities. Used to describe true *italics*, as opposed to slanted *obliques* of *Roman* forms.

Deboss
As *emboss* but recessed into the *substrate*.

Descender
The part of a letter that falls below the baseline.

Die cut
Special shapes cut into a *substrate* by a steel rule.

Display type
Large and/or distinctive type intended to attract the eye. Specifically cut to be viewed from a distance.

Dot gain
Dot gain describes the enlarging of ink dots on the printing stock and is something that occurs naturally as the ink is absorbed into the stock.

Down stroke
The heavy *stroke* in a type character.

Drop capital
A capital letter set in a larger *point* size and aligned with the top of the first line.

Ear
Decorative flourish on the upper right side of the 'g' *bowl*.

Em
Unit of measurement derived from the width of the square body of the cast upper case 'M'. An em equals the size of a given type, i.e. the em of 10 *point* type is 10 points.

Emboss
A design stamped without ink or foil giving a raised surface.

En
Unit of measurement equal to half of one *em*.

Extended
A wider version of the *Roman* cut.

Eye
A *counter*, specifically of 'e'.

Font
The physical attributes needed to make a typeface, be it film, metal, wood or *PostScript* information.

Foot
Serif at the bottom of the *stem* that sits on the *baseline*.

Geometric
Sans serif fonts that are based on geometric shapes identifiable by round 'O' and 'Q' letters.

Golden Section / golden ratio
A division in the ratio 8:13 that produces harmonious proportions.

Gothic
A *typeface* without *serifs*. Also called sans serif or lineale.

Gravure
A high volume *intaglio* printing process in which the printing area is etched into the printing plate.

Hairline
The thinnest *stroke* in a *typeface* that has varying widths. Also refers to a 0.25pt line, the thinnest line that can be confidently produced by printing processes.

Hand drawn
Typography that is hand made.

Hierarchy
A logical, organized and visual guide for text headings that indicates different levels of importance.

Hook
Serif at the top of a *stem*.

Ink trapping
The adjustment of areas of colour, text or shapes to account for misregistration on the printing press by overlapping them.

Intaglio
A technique that describes the printing of an image from a recessed design that is incised or etched into the surface of a plate. The ink lies recessed below the surface of the plate, transfers to the stock under pressure and stands in relief on the stock.

Italic
A version of the *Roman* cut that angles to the right at 7-20 degrees.

Kerning
The removal of unwanted space between letters.

Kerning pairs
Letter combinations that frequently need to be kerned.

Knockout
Where an underlying colour has a gap inserted where another colour would overprint it. The bottom colour is knocked out to prevent colour mixing.

Leading
The space between lines of type measured from *baseline* to baseline. It is expressed in *points* and is a term derived from hot metal type printing when strips of lead were placed between lines of type to provide line spacing.

Leg
The lower, down sloping stroke of the 'K', 'k' and 'R'. Sometimes used for the *tail* of a 'Q'.

Legibility
The ability to distinguish one letter from another due to characteristics inherent in the *typeface* design.

Ligatures
The joining of two or three separate characters to form a single unit to avoid interference between certain letter combinations.

Light
A version of the *Roman* cut with a lighter *stroke*.

Lining numerals
Lining figures are numerals that share the same height and rest on the *baseline*.

Link
The part that joins the two *counters* of the double-storey 'g'.

Loop
The enclosed or partially enclosed lower *counter* in a *Roman* e.g. double-storey 'g'. Sometimes used to describe the *cursive* 'p' and 'b'.

Lower case
See *Minuscules*.

Majuscules
Capital letters. Also called upper case.

Meanline
Imaginary line that runs across the tops of non-ascending characters.

Measure
The length of a line of text expressed in *picas*.

Minuscules
Characters originated from the Carolingian letters. Also called *lower case*.

Monospaced
Where each character occupies a space with the same width.

Oblique
A slanted version of *Roman* whose letterforms are essentially those of the Roman form. Mistakenly called *italics*.

Old Style
Old Style, Antiqua, Ancient, Renaissance, Baroque, Venetian or Garalde is a typeface style developed by Renaissance typographers that was based on Roman inscriptions. It was created to replace the Blackletter type and is characterized by low stroke contrast, bracketed *serifs*, and a left inclining stress.

Old Style figures
Numerals that vary in height and do not sit on the same baseline.

Overprint
Where one printing ink is printed over another.

Pica
A measurement for specifying line lengths. One pica is 12 *points* (UK/US) or 4.22mm. There are six picas to an inch.

Point system
The measurement for specifying typographical dimensions. The British and American point is 1/72 of an inch. The European Didot system provides similar size values.

PostScript
A page description language used by laser printers and on-screen graphics systems.

Quad
A non-printing metal block used as a spacing device.

Readability
The overall visual representation of the text narrative.

Registration
The alignment of printing plates to create a cohesive image or reproduction.

Roman
The basic letterform.

Sans serif
A font without decorative serifs. Typically with little stroke thickness variation, a larger x-height and no stress in rounded strokes.

Script
A *typeface* designed to imitate handwriting.

Serif
A small *stroke* at the end of a main vertical or horizontal stroke. Also used as a classification for typefaces that contain such decorative rounded, pointed, square, or *slab serif* finishing strokes.

Shoulder or body
The arch formed on the 'h'.

Slab serif
A font with heavy, squared-off finishing *strokes*, low contrast and few curves.

Small caps
Small caps are *majuscules* that are close in size to the *minuscules* of a given *typeface*.

Spine
The left to right curving *stroke* in 'S' and 's'.

Spur
The end of the curved part of 'C' or 'S'.

Stem
The main vertical or diagonal *stroke* of a letter.

Stress
The direction in which a curved *stroke* changes weight.

Stroke
The diagonal portion of letterforms such as 'N', 'M', or 'Y'. *Stems, bars, arms, bowls* etc. are collectively referred to as *strokes*.

Substrate
Any surface or material that is to be printed upon.

Surprint
See *Overprint*.

Tail
Descending *stroke* on 'Q', 'K' or 'R'. *Descenders* on 'g', 'j', 'p', 'q', and 'y' may also be called tails.

Terminal
A curve such as a *tail, link, ear* or *loop*, also called finial. A ball terminal combines a tail dot or circular stroke with a hook at the end of a *tail* or *arm*. A beak terminal is a sharp *spur* at the end of an arm.

Tracking
The adjustable amount of space between letters.

Typeface
The letters, numbers and punctuation marks of a type design.

Typeface family
A series of *typefaces* sharing common characteristics but with different sizes and weights.

Type styles
The different visual appearances of typefaces.

Uppercase
See *Majuscules*.

Upstroke
The finer stroke of a type character.

Vertex
The angle formed at the bottom where the left and right *strokes* meet, such as with the 'V'.

X-height
The height of the lowercase 'x' of a given typeface.

index

Compiled by Indexing Specialists (UK) Ltd

contacts

Lynne Elvins/Naomi Goulder

Working with ethics

The Fundamentals
of Typography

Ethical:
aware-
ness/
reflect-
ion/
debate

Publisher's note

The subject of ethics is not new, yet its consideration within the applied visual arts is perhaps not as prevalent as it might be. Our aim here is to help a new generation of students, educators and practitioners find a methodology for structuring their thoughts and reflections in this vital area.

AVA Publishing hopes that these **Working with ethics** pages provide a platform for consideration and a flexible method for incorporating ethical concerns in the work of educators, students and professionals. Our approach consists of four parts:

The **introduction** is intended to be an accessible snapshot of the ethical landscape, both in terms of historical development and current dominant themes.

The **framework** positions ethical consideration into four areas and poses questions about the practical implications that might occur. Marking your response to each of these questions on the scale shown will allow your reactions to be further explored by comparison.

The **case study** sets out a real project and then poses some ethical questions for further consideration. This is a focus point for a debate rather than a critical analysis so there are no predetermined right or wrong answers.

A selection of **further reading** for you to consider areas of particular interest in more detail.

Introduction

Ethics is a complex subject that interlaces the idea of responsibilities to society with a wide range of considerations relevant to the character and happiness of the individual. It concerns virtues of compassion, loyalty and strength, but also of confidence, imagination, humour and optimism. As introduced in ancient Greek philosophy, the fundamental ethical question is: *what should I do?* How we might pursue a 'good' life not only raises moral concerns about the effects of our actions on others, but also personal concerns about our own integrity.

In modern times the most important and controversial questions in ethics have been the moral ones. With growing populations and improvements in mobility and communications, it is not surprising that considerations about how to structure our lives together on the planet should come to the forefront. For visual artists and communicators, it should be no surprise that these considerations will enter into the creative process.

Some ethical considerations are already enshrined in government laws and regulations or in professional codes of conduct. For example, plagiarism and breaches of confidentiality can be punishable offences. Legislation in various nations makes it unlawful to exclude people with disabilities from accessing information or spaces. The trade of ivory as a material has been banned in many countries. In these cases, a clear line has been drawn under what is unacceptable.

But most ethical matters remain open to debate, among experts and lay-people alike, and in the end we have to make our own choices on the basis of our own guiding principles or values. Is it more ethical to work for a charity than for a commercial company? Is it unethical to create something that others find ugly or offensive?

Specific questions such as these may lead to other questions that are more abstract. For example, is it only effects on humans (and what they care about) that are important, or might effects on the natural world require attention too?

Is promoting ethical consequences justified even when it requires ethical sacrifices along the way? Must there be a single unifying theory of ethics (such as the Utilitarian thesis that the right course of action is always the one that leads to the greatest happiness of the greatest number), or might there always be many different ethical values that pull a person in various directions?

As we enter into ethical debate and engage with these dilemmas on a personal and professional level, we may change our views or change our view of others. The real test though is whether, as we reflect on these matters, we change the way we act as well as the way we think. Socrates, the 'father' of philosophy, proposed that people will naturally do 'good' if they know what is right. But this point might only lead us to yet another question: *how do we know what is right?*

You

What are your ethical beliefs?

Central to everything you do will be your attitude to people and issues around you. For some people, their ethics are an active part of the decisions they make every day as a consumer, a voter or a working professional. Others may think about ethics very little and yet this does not automatically make them unethical. Personal beliefs, lifestyle, politics, nationality, religion, gender, class or education can all influence your ethical viewpoint.

Using the scale, where would you place yourself? What do you take into account to make your decision? Compare results with your friends or colleagues.

Your client

What are your terms?

Working relationships are central to whether ethics can be embedded into a project, and your conduct on a day-to-day basis is a demonstration of your professional ethics. The decision with the biggest impact is whom you choose to work with in the first place. Cigarette companies or arms traders are often-cited examples when talking about where a line might be drawn, but rarely are real situations so extreme. At what point might you turn down a project on ethical grounds and how much does the reality of having to earn a living affect your ability to choose?

Using the scale, where would you place a project? How does this compare to your personal ethical level?

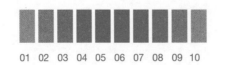

01 02 03 04 05 06 07 08 09 10

01 02 03 04 05 06 07 08 09 10

Your specifications
What are the impacts of your materials?

In relatively recent times, we are learning that many natural materials are in short supply. At the same time, we are increasingly aware that some man-made materials can have harmful, long-term effects on people or the planet. How much do you know about the materials that you use? Do you know where they come from, how far they travel and under what conditions they are obtained? When your creation is no longer needed, will it be easy and safe to recycle? Will it disappear without a trace? Are these considerations your responsibility or are they out of your hands?

Using the scale, mark how ethical your material choices are.

Your creation
What is the purpose of your work?

Between you, your colleagues and an agreed brief, what will your creation achieve? What purpose will it have in society and will it make a positive contribution? Should your work result in more than commercial success or industry awards? Might your creation help save lives, educate, protect or inspire? Form and function are two established aspects of judging a creation, but there is little consensus on the obligations of visual artists and communicators toward society, or the role they might have in solving social or environmental problems. If you want recognition for being the creator, how responsible are you for what you create and where might that responsibility end?

Using the scale, mark how ethical the purpose of your work is.

01 02 03 04 05 06 07 08 09 10

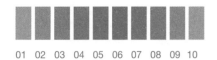

01 02 03 04 05 06 07 08 09 10

An aspect of typography that may raise ethical issues is its capacity to make information accessible or understandable to the reader. Creative use of typography can emphasise meaning and embed emotion in words. In this way, typography can facilitate verbal and visual communication, and in turn give rise to fundamental questions about the role of a given piece of text.

Will the text instruct, inform or helpfully guide the receiver towards beneficial information of some kind? Or might it confuse, frighten or alienate all but a select few? Does a typographer have a responsibility to always be as clear, informative and legible as possible? Or are there occasions where the decorative treatment of script is far more important than the ability to read the words? How much responsibility should the typographer assume for the message, as well as for the means by which it is delivered?

Graffiti has been found around the world and throughout history, from the catacombs of Rome to the Mayan temple walls of Tikal in Mesoamerica. Graffiti found in Pompeii, with its messages of political rhetoric or Latin curses, provides us with insights into the daily lives of people during the first century. Graffiti continues to tell us about life today, as well as directly reflecting the writer's views of society.

In France during the student protests and general strike of May 1968, revolutionary anarchist and situationist slogans covered the walls of Paris, articulating the spirit of the age. In the US, around the same time, street gangs were using graffiti as a means to mark territory. Signatures or 'tags', rather than slogans, were used by writers such as TOPCAT 126 and COOL EARL. CORNBREAD, credited by some as the father of modern graffiti, began his career by writing 'Cornbread loves Cynthia' all over his school. In the early 1970s, graffiti moved to New York and writers such as TAKI 183 began to add their street number to their nickname. Tags began to take on a calligraphic appearance in order to stand out, and also began to grow in size and include thick outlines. Bubble lettering was initially popular before 'wildstyle' – a complicated creation of interlocking letters using lots of arrows and connections – came to define the art of graffiti.

The use of graffiti as a portrayal of rebellious urban style made it attractive to creatives operating within mainstream culture. In 2001, fashion designer and artist Stephen Sprouse, in collaboration with fellow designer Marc Jacobs, designed a limited-edition line of Louis Vuitton bags that featured graffiti scrawled over the company's monogrammed pattern.

Despite the fact that graffiti has now become both a familiar and accepted artistic form within everyday society, it remains controversial. There is a clear distinction between graffiti employed typographically by a designer or artist, to graffiti that is applied to either public or private property. In most countries, defacing property without permission is deemed to be vandalism and is therefore punishable by law. Governments spend vast sums of public money removing graffiti. A 1995 study by the National Graffiti Information Network estimated that the cost of cleaning up graffiti in the US amounted annually to approximately USD$8 billion.

If it is illegal, is it also unethical to graffiti on someone else's property?

Are companies exploiting graffiti if they use it to sell commercial goods?

Would you be prepared to be imprisoned to communicate a message?

A word is not a crystal, transparent and unchanged; it is the skin of a living thought, and may vary greatly in color and content according to the circumstances and the time in which it is used.

Oliver Wendell Holmes Jr

AIGA
Design Business and Ethics
2007, AIGA

Eaton, Marcia Muelder
Aesthetics and the Good Life
1989, Associated University Press

Ellison, David
Ethics and Aesthetics in European Modernist Literature:
From the Sublime to the Uncanny
2001, Cambridge University Press

Fenner, David E W (Ed)
Ethics and the Arts:
An Anthology
1995, Garland Reference Library of Social Science

Gini, Al and Marcoux, Alexei M
Case Studies in Business Ethics
2005, Prentice Hall

McDonough, William and Braungart, Michael
Cradle to Cradle:
Remaking the Way We Make Things
2002, North Point Press

Papanek, Victor
Design for the Real World:
Making to Measure
1972, Thames & Hudson

United Nations Global Compact
The Ten Principles
www.unglobalcompact.org/AboutTheGC/TheTenPrinciples/index.html